# A SEASON I...

## 16 Quilt Patterns and a Cozy Cabin Full of Inspiration

**EDYTA SITAR** ✳ FOR LAUNDRY BASKET QUILTS

Copyright© 2021 by Laundry Basket Quilts
Quilt Designs by Edyta Sitar

This book was produced and published by
Sitar Family Traditions, LLC,
DBA: Laundry Basket Quilts
Oxnard, CA
www.LaundryBasketQuilts.com

**Publisher:** Sitar Family Traditions, LLC,
Laundry Basket Quilts
**Quilt Design:** Edyta Sitar
**Graphic Designer:** Angie Haupert Hoogensen
**Technical Illustrators:** Lisa Christensen,
Sandy Loi, and Michael Sitar
**Styled Photography:** Mary Adams and Edyta Sitar
**Photographer:** Neil Koehn

For questions or concerns regarding editorial
content, contact Laundry Basket Quilts at
www.laundrybasketquilts.com.

DISTRIBUTOR
To order copies of this book for wholesale, retail,
or individual sale, contact:

**Martingale**
Create with Confidence

**Martingale**
18939 120th Ave. NE, Suite 101
Bothell, WA 98011-9511 USA
ShopMartingale.com

ISBN 978-1-68356-164-4
Library of Congress Cataloging-in-Publication
Data is available upon request.

Printed in Hong Kong
26 25 24 23 22        8 7 6 5 4 3 2

# contents

## dedication

To the important men in my life—my father, Michal, my husband, Michael, and my son, Michael. My dad taught me the importance of the basic joys in life. Together my husband and I have built a home and a family. And my son has brought untold joy to my life as I watch him build his life as an adult. I am truly blessed to have these three men in my life and my heart.

# introduction

Reflecting on the past year and the time apart many of us spent from friends and family, it was easy to feel restless staying home and traveling less. But as the months passed, I also was able to find a silver lining. I'm thankful for the extra time I spent with my family and within my own home. And I bet many of you were too. As a quilter, I enjoyed reflecting on the simple pleasures of creating and was very much reminded by how little it takes to entertain myself. Surrounded by fabric, some thread, and needles, I'm happy to spend time (all day even) at my sewing machine. Quilting is not just my entertainment, but an escape when I need a break.

Looking for calm in uncertain times, I also took pleasure in a familiar color palette. Blue is one of my favorite colors, and a favorite for many others too. Two-color quilts in blue and white are relaxing to my soul. So I immersed myself in fabric and traveled to far-away places in my mind. I translated favorite destinations into quilts with familiar names. Missing snowy days on the mountain trails, I stitched up a flurry of snowflakes. With more time in the sewing room, I hope you also rediscovered the joy of letting your mind wander and felt creativity bubbling up as you quilted.

I hope the pages that follow fill your heart with dreams of a happy future. And I hope the only difficulty you have is in choosing which pattern to make first!

—Edyta

# gallery of inspiration

When your heart is full of possibilities for what could be, your mind opens up to the magic of being a maker. Beautiful images feed our souls. As quilters we look at pictures and our minds begin to race with ideas of who we can make a quilt for or how it will look in our home. For this gallery, I chose a winter cabin theme to signify the cozy heart of a home, something I've come to appreciate now more than ever. My hope is that you will turn to these pages time and again to imagine these quilts sparkling in your decor, wrapped around the shoulders of your loved ones, or covering your lap on a chilly night. Enjoy!

*Patterns for quilts shown in the gallery but not included in the project section of this book may be found for individual sale at LaundryBasketQuilts.com.*

Casually draping quilts over a railing is a welcoming display and invites guests to wrap up in a quilt to get cozy.

Personalize a showstopper such as *Simple Life* by including the appliqués most meaningful to you.

As quilters, decorating our homes with quilts and accessories makes us feel comfortable and happy. What's your home's coziest spot?

Look for joy in the simple things as you wander through and around your home. Let the shapes you see inside and outdoors inspire you.

Let me share a time-saving secret. *Family Tree* uses Laundry Basket Quilts prefused laser-cut appliqué shapes.

In a spot where a wall hanging won't fit, drape a quilt on an artful ladder instead.

Looking for other unique quilt displays? An over-the-door wreath hanger and a ribbon to gather the top of your quilt become the perfect duo to show off *First Dance*.

Even without playing in the snow,
I find my own one-of-a-kind everlasting
snowflakes. I hope you do too!

Each of my quilts tells a story. Some stories are about places I remember, others are about feelings I want to express. What stories do your quilts tell?

Mixing appliqué and patchwork is a perfect pairing for me, like fresh snowfall and the mountains.

Take time to ponder. When you pause to look around and wonder, your mind can unleash new expressions through your quilting.

What do you dream about when you're nestled under a quilt? Might it be your next project or a new idea for decorating with quilts?

Always take the chance to learn something new—in quilting, at home, and in life. Experimenting with the unknown helps you grow.

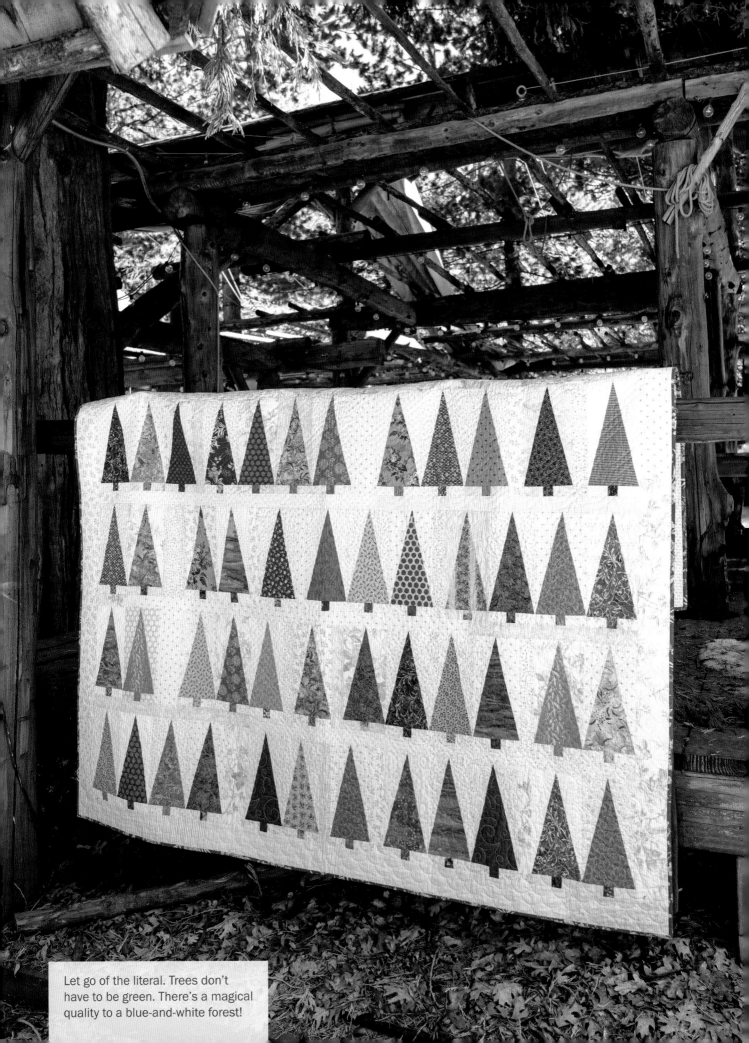

Let go of the literal. Trees don't have to be green. There's a magical quality to a blue-and-white forest!

What sets your heart on fire?
Is it the simplicity of a single quilt?
Is it a grouping of quilts nestled
together, or how about a perfect
pair? Listen to your heart and
find more ways to speak to it
through your quilts.

Our paths on this quilting journey are different from one another, but the common thread is the warmth of quilts.

Make beautiful things so that your home and family are surrounded by the love you stitch into every patch.

# alaska

The beauty of Alaska is in its stunning snow-capped mountains,
icy blue waters, twinkling bright night skies, and of course its people.
This quilt celebrates them all.

**Quilt is 71½" × 71½"**

# fabric requirements

**Blocks:**
- 2½ yards of Print 1 (light)
- 1⅓ yards of Print 2 (medium light)
- 1⅓ yards of Print 3 (light blue)
- ¼ yard of Print 4 (medium blue)
- 1¼ yards of Print 5 (dark blue)
- ⅔ yard of Print 6 (very dark blue)

**Border:** 1⅛ yards of light print
**Binding:** ⅔ yard of blue print
**Backing:** 4¼ yards
**Batting:** 78" × 78"
**Optional:** Creative Grids Alaska Ruler (CGRLBQ1)

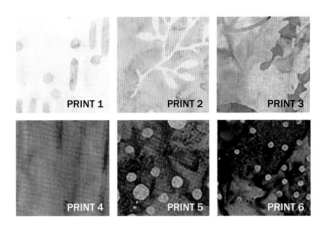

PRINT 1   PRINT 2   PRINT 3

PRINT 4   PRINT 5   PRINT 6

# fabric cutting

Please read all instructions before cutting. WOF designates the width of fabric from selvedge to selvedge (approximately 42" wide). Cutting is listed by template for each fabric. For ease in assembly, keep pieces separated by print until ready to begin each block's assembly. Templates are on page 39.

**Print 1** (light)
- 5—2⅞" × WOF strips
  from those strips, cut 104 of Template B
- 12—5⅛" × WOF strips
  from those strips, cut 156 of Template C
- 3—3½" × WOF strips
  from those strips, cut 52 of Template D

**Print 2** (medium light)
- 1—2½" × WOF strip
  from that strip, cut 4 of Template A
- 5— 2⅞" × WOF strips
  from those strips, cut 104 of Template B
- 3—5⅛" × WOF strips
  from those strips, cut 32 of Template C
- 3—3½" × WOF strips
  from those strips, cut 52 of Template D

**Print 3** (light blue)
- 8—2¼" × WOF strips
  from those strips, cut 60 of Template A
- 2—2⅞" × WOF strips
  from those strips, cut 48 of Template B
- 3—5⅛" × WOF strips
  from those strips, cut 32 of Template C
- 1—3½" × WOF strip
  from that strip, cut 20 of Template D

**Print 4** (medium blue)
- 1— 5⅛" × WOF strip
  from that strip, cut 12 of Template C

**Print 5** (dark blue)
- 10—2¼" × WOF strips
  from those strips, cut 80 of Template A
- 2—2⅞" × WOF strips
  from those strips, cut 32 of Template B
- 1—5⅛" × WOF strip
  from that strip, cut 8 of Template C
- 1—3½" × WOF strip
  from that strip, cut 16 of Template D

**Print 6** (very dark blue)
- 1—2¼" × WOF strip
  from that strip, cut 8 of Template A
- 1—2⅞" × WOF strip
  from that strip, cut 16 of Template B
- 3—3½" × WOF strips
  from those strip, cut 56 of Template D

**Border:**
- 8—4½" × WOF strips

Sew two strips end-to-end to make a long strip.
Make 4 long strips. Then cut from those strips:
- 2— 4½" × 71½" long border strips
- 2— 4½" × 63½" short border strips

**Binding:**
- 8—2½" × WOF strips

# construction

1 Each block will be made four times, except Block 13, which is made only once. Press toward the darker fabric unless a directional arrow is indicated on the illustration.

## BLOCK 1

 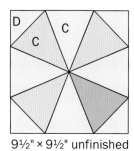

9½" × 9½" unfinished

To make four of Block 1, you will need:
**Print 1**: 16 D light triangles; 16 C light wedges
**Print 2**: 12 C medium light wedges
**Print 4**: four C medium blue wedges

(A) Join one C light wedge, one C medium light wedge, and one D light triangle to make Unit A. Repeat to make 12 total of Unit A.
(B) Join one C light wedge, one C medium blue wedge, and one D light triangle to make Unit B. Repeat to make four total of Unit B.
(C) Sew together three of Unit A and one Unit B as shown to make Block 1; press. Repeat to make a total of four of Block 1.

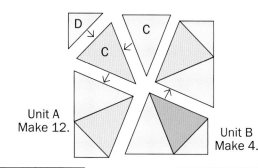

Unit A
Make 12.

Unit B
Make 4.

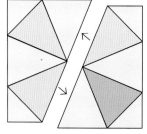 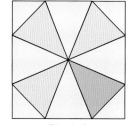

Block 1
9½" × 9½" unfinished
Make 4.

## BLOCK 2

 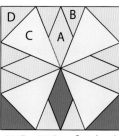

9½" × 9½" unfinished

To make four of Block 2, you will need:
**Print 1**: 16 C light wedges
**Print 2**: eight D medium light triangles and 24 B medium light half-diamonds
**Print 3**: 12 A light blue diamonds and eight B light blue half-diamonds
**Print 6**: four A very dark blue diamonds and eight D very dark blue triangles

(A) Join one A light blue diamond, two B medium light half-diamonds, one C light wedge, and one D medium light triangle to make Unit A. Repeat to make eight total of Unit A.
(B) Join one A light blue diamond, two B medium light half-diamonds, one C light wedge, and one D very dark blue triangle to make Unit B. Repeat to make four total of Unit B.
(C) Join one A very dark blue diamond, two B light blue half-diamonds, one C light wedge, and one D very dark blue triangle to make Unit C. Repeat to make four total of Unit C.

(D) Sew together two of Unit A, one Unit B, and one Unit C as shown to make Block 2; press. Repeat to make a total of four of Block 2.

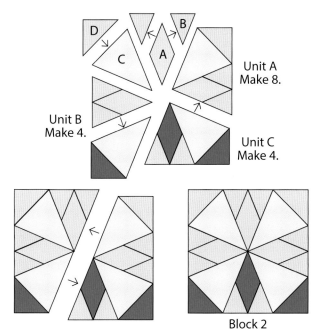

Unit A Make 8.

Unit B Make 4.

Unit C Make 4.

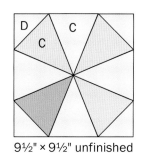

Block 2
9½" × 9½" unfinished
Make 4.

(D) Sew together two of Unit A, one Unit B, and one Unit C as shown to make Block 3; press. Repeat to make a total of four of Block 3.

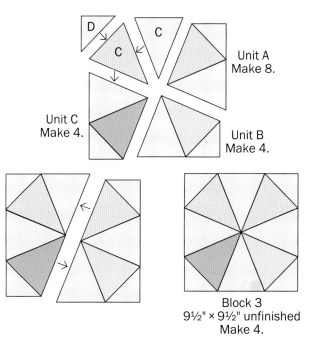

Unit A Make 8.

Unit C Make 4.

Unit B Make 4.

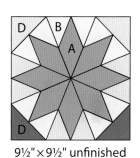

Block 3
9½" × 9½" unfinished
Make 4.

## BLOCK 3

![Block 3 photo and diagram]

9½" × 9½" unfinished

To make four of Block 3, you will need:
**Print 1:** 16 D light triangles and 16 C light wedges
**Print 2:** eight C medium light wedges
**Print 3:** four C light blue wedges
**Print 4:** four C medium blue wedges

(A) Join one C light wedge, one C medium light wedge, and one D light triangle to make Unit A. Repeat to make eight total of Unit A.
(B) Join one C light wedge, one C light blue wedge, and one D light triangle to make Unit B. Repeat to make four total of Unit B.
(C) Join one C light wedge, one C medium blue wedge, and one D light triangle to make Unit C. Repeat to make four total of Unit C.

## BLOCK 4

![Block 4 photo and diagram]

9½" × 9½" unfinished

To make four of Block 4, you will need:
**Print 1:** 40 B light half-diamonds
**Print 2:** eight D medium light triangles and 24 B medium light half-diamonds
**Print 5:** 32 A dark blue diamonds
**Print 6:** eight D very dark blue triangles

(A) Join two A dark blue diamonds, four B light half-diamonds, and one D medium light triangle to make Unit A. Repeat to make four total of Unit A.
(B) Join two A dark blue diamonds, two B medium light half-diamonds, two B light half-diamonds, and one D medium light triangle to make Unit B. Repeat to make four total of Unit B.
(C) Join two A dark blue diamonds, two B medium light half-diamonds, two B light half-diamonds, and one D very dark blue triangle to make Unit C. Repeat to make eight total of Unit C.

(D) Sew together one Unit A, one Unit B, and two of Unit C as shown to make Block 4; press. Repeat to make a total of four of Block 4.

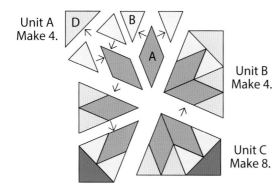

Unit A
Make 4.

Unit B
Make 4.

Unit C
Make 8.

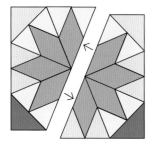

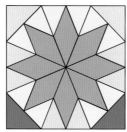

Block 4
9½"×9½" unfinished
Make 4.

## BLOCK 5

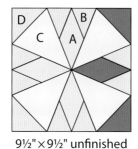

9½"×9½" unfinished

To make four of Block 5, you will need:

**Print 1:** 16 C light wedges

**Print 2:** eight D medium light triangles and 24 B medium light half-diamonds

**Print 3:** 12 A light blue diamonds and eight B light blue half-diamonds

**Print 6:** four A very dark blue diamonds and eight D very dark blue triangles

(A) Join one A light blue diamond, two B medium light half-diamonds, one C light wedge, and one D medium light triangle to make Unit A. Repeat to make eight total of Unit A.

(B) Join one A very dark blue diamond, two B light blue half-diamonds, one C light wedge, and one D very dark blue triangle to make Unit B. Repeat to make four total of Unit B.

(C) Join one A light blue diamond, two B medium light half-diamonds, one C light wedge, and one D very dark blue triangle to make Unit C. Repeat to make four total of Unit C.

(D) Join two of Unit A, one Unit B, and one Unit C as shown to make Block 5; press. Repeat to make a total of four of Block 5.

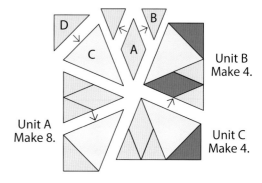

Unit B
Make 4.

Unit A
Make 8.

Unit C
Make 4.

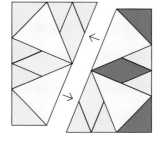

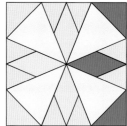

Block 5
9½"×9½" unfinished
Make 4.

## BLOCK 6

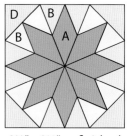

9½"×9½" unfinished

To make four of Block 6, you will need:

**Print 1:** 32 B light half-diamonds

**Print 2:** 16 D medium light triangles

**Print 3:** 32 B light blue half-diamonds

**Print 5:** 32 A dark blue diamonds

(A) Join two A dark blue diamonds, 2 B light half-diamonds, 2 B light blue half-diamonds, and 1 D medium light triangle to make Unit A. Repeat to make 16 total of Unit A.

(B) Join four of Unit A as shown to make Block 6; press. Repeat to make a total of four of Block 6.

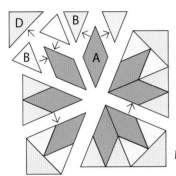

Unit A
Make 16.

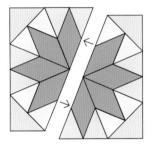

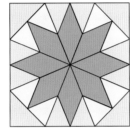

Block 6
9½" × 9½" unfinished
Make 4.

## BLOCK 7

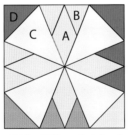

9½" × 9½" unfinished

To make four of Block 7, you will need:

**Print 1:** 16 C light wedges

**Print 2:** 16 B medium light half-diamonds

**Print 3:** 16 A light blue diamonds and four D light blue triangles

**Print 5:** eight B dark blue half-diamonds and four D dark blue triangles

**Print 6:** eight B very dark blue half-diamonds and eight D very dark blue triangles

(A) Join one A light blue diamond, two B medium light half-diamonds, one C light wedge, and one D very dark blue triangle to make Unit A. Repeat to make four total of Unit A.

(B) Join one A light blue diamond, two B very dark blue half-diamonds, one C light wedge, and one D very dark blue triangle to make Unit B. Repeat to make four total of Unit B.

(C) Join one A light blue diamond, two B dark blue half-diamonds, one C light wedge, and one D light blue triangle to make Unit C. Repeat to make four total of Unit C.

(D) Join one A light blue diamond, two B medium light half-diamonds, one C light wedge, and one D dark blue triangle to make Unit D. Repeat to make four total of Unit D.

(E) Join one Unit A, one Unit B, one Unit C, and one Unit D as shown to make Block 7; press. Repeat to make a total of four of Block 7.

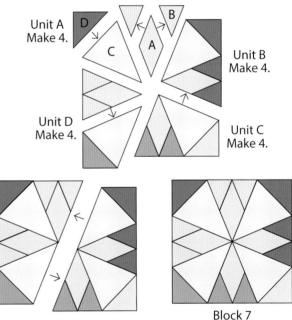

Block 7
9½" × 9½" unfinished
Make 4.

"When you finish a set of blocks, clearly mark them with a tag or place them in a bag with the block number. That will make assembling the rows easier." –Edyta

## BLOCK 8

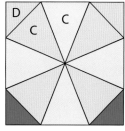

9½" × 9½" unfinished

To make four of Block 8, you will need:
**Print 1:** 16 C light wedges
**Print 2:** eight D medium light triangles
**Print 3:** 16 C light blue wedges
**Print 6:** eight D very dark blue triangles

(A) Join one C light wedge, one C light blue wedge, and one D medium light triangle D to make Unit A. Repeat to make eight total of Unit A.
(B) Join one C light wedge, one C light blue wedge, and one D very dark blue triangle to make Unit B. Repeat to make eight total of Unit B.
(C) Sew together two of Unit A and two of Unit B as shown to make Block 8; press. Repeat to make a total of four of Block 8.

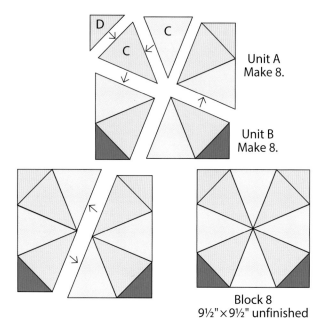

Unit A
Make 8.

Unit B
Make 8.

Block 8
9½" × 9½" unfinished
Make 4.

## BLOCK 9

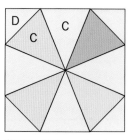

9½" × 9½" unfinished

To make four of Block 9, you will need:
**Print 1:** 16 D light triangles and 16 C light wedges
**Print 2:** 8 C medium light wedges
**Print 3:** 4 C light blue wedges
**Print 4:** 4 C medium blue wedges

(A) Join one C light wedge, one C medium light wedge, and one D light triangle to make Unit A. Repeat to make eight total of Unit A.
(B) Join one C light wedge, one C medium blue wedge, and one D light triangle to make Unit B. Repeat to make four total of Unit B.
(C) Join one C light wedge, one C light blue wedge, and one D light triangle to make Unit C. Repeat to make four total of Unit C.
(D) Sew together two of Unit A, one Unit B, and one Unit C to make Block 9; press. Repeat to make a total of four of Block 9.

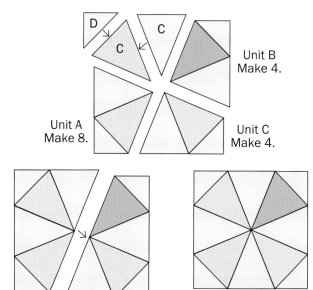

Unit B
Make 4.

Unit A
Make 8.

Unit C
Make 4.

Block 9
9½" × 9½" unfinished
Make 4.

## BLOCK 10

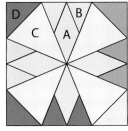

9½" × 9½" unfinished

To make four of Block 10, you will need:

**Print 1:** 16 C light wedges

**Print 2:** 16 B medium light half-diamonds

**Print 3:** 16 A light blue diamonds and 4 D light blue triangles

**Print 5:** 8 B dark blue half-diamonds and 4 D dark blue triangles

**Print 6:** 8 B very dark blue half-diamonds and 8 D very dark blue triangles

(A) Join one A light blue diamond, two B medium light half-diamonds, one C light wedge, and one D very dark blue triangle to make Unit A. Repeat to make eight total of Unit A.

(B) Join one A light blue diamond A, two B dark blue half-diamonds, one C light wedge, and one D dark blue triangle to make Unit B. Repeat to make four total of Unit B.

(C) Join one A light blue diamond, two B very dark blue half-diamonds, one C light wedge, and one D light blue triangle to make Unit C. Repeat to make four total of Unit C.

(D) Sew together two of Unit A, one Unit B, and one Unit C to make Block 10; press. Repeat to make a total of four of Block 10.

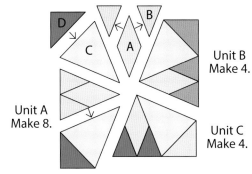

Unit A
Make 8.

Unit B
Make 4.

Unit C
Make 4.

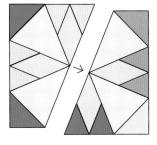
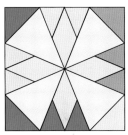

Block 10
9½" × 9½" unfinished
Make 4.

## BLOCK 11

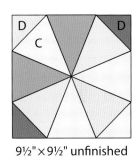

9½" × 9½" unfinished

To make four of Block 11, you will need:

**Print 1:** 4 D light triangles and 12 C light wedges

**Print 2:** 4 C medium light wedges and 4 D medium triangles

**Print 3:** 8 C light blue wedges

**Print 5:** 8 C dark blue wedges

**Print 6:** 8 D very dark blue triangles

(A) Join one C light wedge, one C dark blue wedge, and one D medium light triangle to make Unit A. Repeat to make a four total of Unit A.

(B) Join one C light blue wedge, one C light wedge, and one D very dark blue triangle to make Unit B. Repeat to make a four total of Unit B.

(C) Join one C medium light wedge, one C light wedge, and one D light triangle to make Unit C. Repeat to make a four total of Unit C.

(D) Join one C light blue wedge, one C dark blue wedge, and one D very dark blue triangle to make Unit D. Repeat to make four total of Unit D.

(E) Sew together one Unit A, one Unit B, one Unit C, and one Unit D to make Block 11; press. Repeat to make a total of four of Block 11.

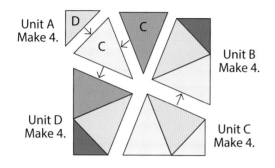

Unit A
Make 4.

Unit B
Make 4.

Unit D
Make 4.

Unit C
Make 4.

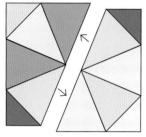

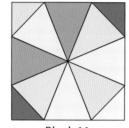

Block 11
9½" × 9½" unfinished
Make 4.

**BLOCK 12**

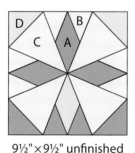

9½" × 9½" unfinished

To make four of Block 12, you will need:

**Print 1:** 16 C light wedges and 24 B light half-diamonds

**Print 3:** 4 A light blue diamonds and 8 D medium triangles

**Print 5:** 12 A dark blue diamonds, 8 D dark blue triangles, and 8 B dark blue half-diamonds

(A) Join one A dark blue diamond, two B light half-diamonds, one C light wedge, and one D dark blue triangle to make Unit A. Repeat to make four total of Unit A.

(B) Join one A dark blue diamond, two B light half-diamonds, one C light wedge, and one C light blue triangle to make Unit B. Repeat to make eight total of Unit B.

(C) Join one A light blue diamond, two B dark blue half-diamonds, one C light wedge, and one D dark blue triangle to make Unit C. Repeat to make four total of Unit C.

(D) Sew together one Unit A, two of Unit B, and one Unit C to make Block 12; press. Repeat to make a total of four of Block 12.

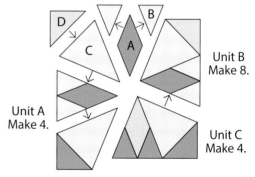

Unit B
Make 8.

Unit A
Make 4.

Unit C
Make 4.

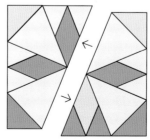

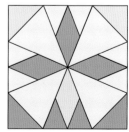

Block 12
9½" × 9½" unfinished
Make 4.

## BLOCK 13—CENTER BLOCK

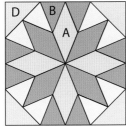

9½" × 9½" unfinished

To make one Block 13, you will need:

**Print 1:** eight B light half-diamonds

**Print 2:** four A medium light diamonds

**Print 3:** four D light blue triangles

**Print 5:** four A dark blue diamonds and eight B dark blue half-diamonds

(A) Join one A dark blue diamond, two B light half-diamonds, one A medium light diamond, two B dark half-diamonds, and one D light blue triangle to make Unit A. Repeat to make four total of Unit A.

(B) Sew together four of Unit A to make Block 13; press.

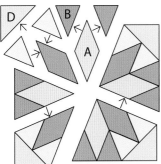

Unit A
Make 4.

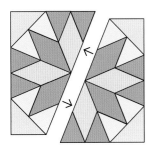

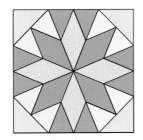

Block 13
9½" × 9½" unfinished
Make 4.

2  Sort the finished blocks for assembly. You should have four EACH of blocks 1–12 and one of Block 13 for the center.

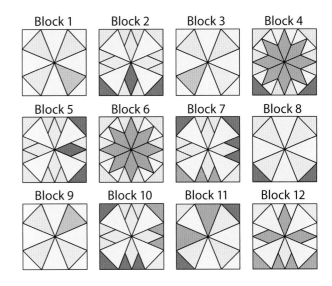

Block 1   Block 2   Block 3   Block 4

Block 5   Block 6   Block 7   Block 8

Block 9   Block 10   Block 11   Block 12

"When you lay out your blocks into rows, experiment with color placement and the rotation of blocks. If you used batik prints, the color variation can be more dense in some areas." –Edyta

## quilt assembly

1 Arrange your blocks as shown in the diagram below, noting the rotation of each block. Sew the blocks into rows, pinning as needed to ensure accuracy. Press seam allowances in opposite directions as shown by the arrows, sew the rows together, and press.

2 **Borders:** Add the 4½" × 63½" short border strips to opposite edges. Add the 4½" × 71½" long border strips to the remaining edges of the quilt top. Press seam allowances towards the outside of the quilt.

3 **Quilting:** Layer the quilt according to the instructions on page 143. Quilt as desired.

4 **Binding:** Use the 2½"-wide blue strips to bind the quilt following the instructions on page 143.

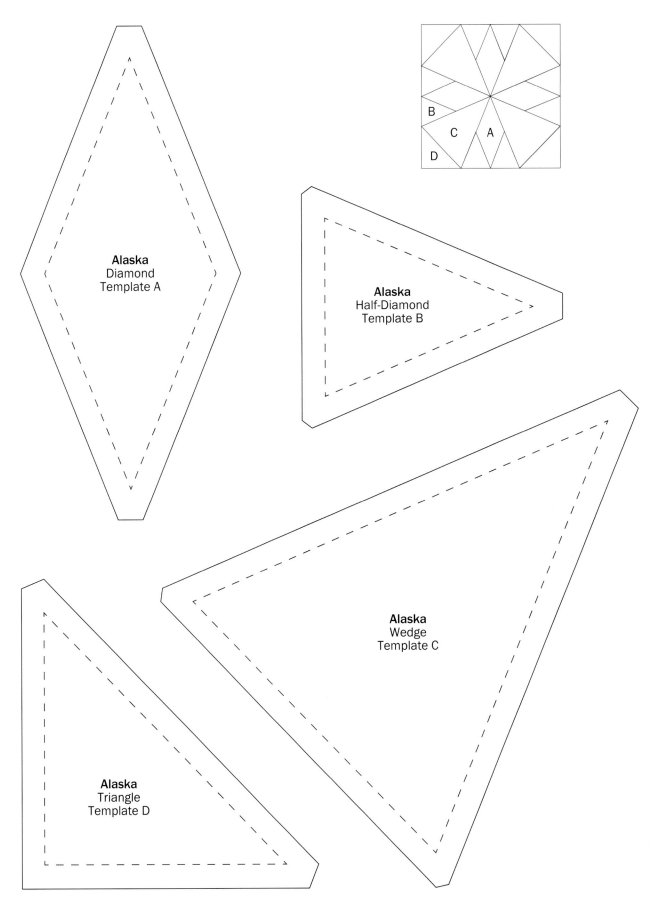

**Alaska**
Diamond
Template A

**Alaska**
Half-Diamond
Template B

**Alaska**
Wedge
Template C

**Alaska**
Triangle
Template D

B

C

A

D

# first dance

Like a moonlight serenade, double Nine Patch blocks dance across a restful light background in a perfectly orchestrated variation of an Irish Chain.

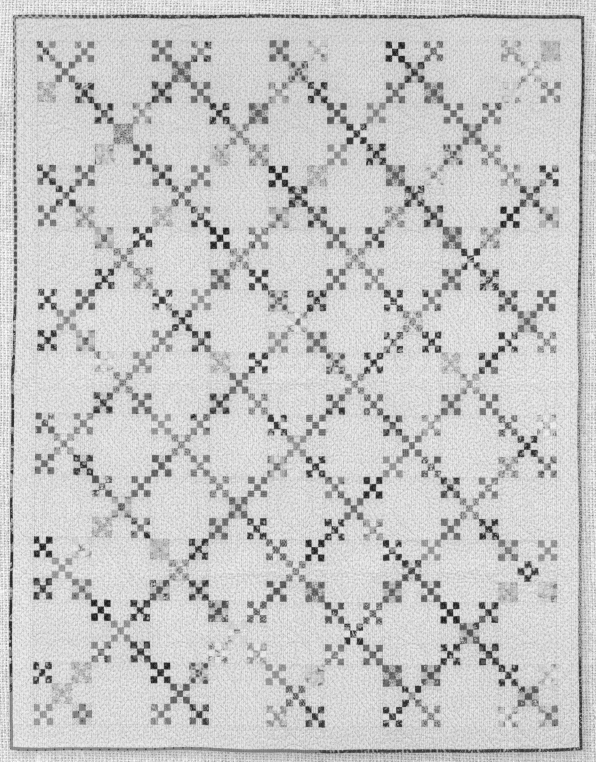

**Quilt is 65¾" × 79¼"**

## fabric requirements

**Nine Patches:**
Blues: 15—fat eighths (9" × 21")*
Lights: 12—fat eighths (9" × 21")
**Background and Borders:**
4¼ yards light fabric
**Binding:** ⅔ yard of blue fabric**
**Backing:** 4¾ yards
**Batting:** 72" × 86"
* For greater variety, consider using a fat-eighth fabric bundle
** The featured quilt has a scrappy binding made with multiple blue prints

## fabric cutting

**Note:** Read assembly directions before cutting patches. Borders are cut to exact length required plus ¼" seam allowance. WOF designates the width of fabric from selvedge to selvedge (approximately 42" wide).

**Nine Patches:**
From the blue fat eighths, cut:
• 85—1¼" × 21" strips
From the light fat eighths, cut:
• 68—1¼" × 21" strips

**Light backgrounds:**
• 10—7¼" × WOF strips
  From those strips, cut:
  49—7¼" × 7¼" squares
• 15—2¾" × WOF strips
  From those strips, cut:
  200—2¾" × 2¾" squares

**Borders:**
• 8—2¾" × WOF strips
Sew strips together end to end, then subcut:
  • 2—2¾" × 74¾" border strips
  • 2—2¾" × 65¾" border strips

**Binding:**
• 8—2½" × WOF strips

*Use a ¼" seam allowance. Press in the direction of the arrows.*

## construction

**1 Nine Patch blocks**

(A) Sew one light and two blue 1¼" × 22" strips together to make an A strip set. Press toward the blue strips. Repeat to make 34 A strip sets total. From each A strip set, cut fifteen 1¼"-wide A segments. Cut a total of 500—1¼" × 2¾" A segments.

(B) Sew one blue and two light 1¼" × 22" strips together to make a B strip set. Press toward the blue strip. Repeat to make 17 B strip sets total. From each B strip set, cut fifteen 1¼"-wide B segments. Cut a total of 250—1¼" × 2¾" B segments.

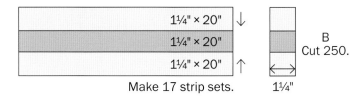

(C) Join two A segments and one B segment as shown to make a Nine Patch block. The block should measure 2¾" × 2¾" including seam allowances. Repeat to make 250 Nine Patch blocks total.

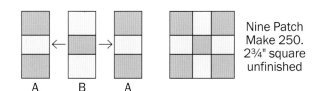

**2** **Assemble the blocks:** Sew four 2¾" light background squares and five Nine Patch blocks together as shown in three rows. Join the rows; press to complete a Double Nine Patch block. The block should be 7¼" × 7¼" including seam allowances. Repeat to make 50 blocks total.

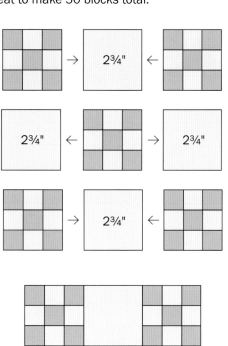

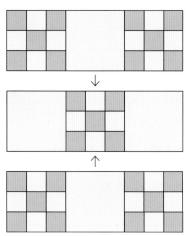

**3** **Assemble the quilt:** Arrange 50 Double Nine Patch blocks and 49—7¼" background squares in rows; sew together. Sew the 11 rows together as shown. The quilt top should measure now 61¼" × 74¾" including seam allowances.

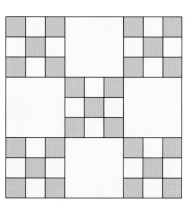

Double Nine Patch Block
Make 50.
7¼" × 7¼" unfinished

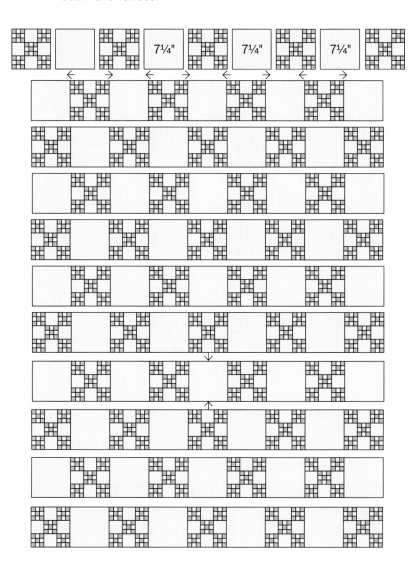

4 Sew a 2¾" × 74¾" border strip to opposite quilt sides as shown. Add the 2¾" × 65¾" border strips to the top and bottom edges.

5 **Quilting:** Layer quilt according to the instructions on page 143. Quilt as desired.

6 **Binding:** Use the 2½"-wide blue strips to bind the quilt following the instructions on page 143.

2¾" × 65¾"

2¾" × 74¾"

2¾" × 74¾"

2¾" × 65¾"

"Remember, a two-color quilt doesn't have to mean just two fabrics. I love scrappy blue-and-white quilts. The more prints the merrier in my quilts!" —Edyta

# pinehurst

Perfectly proportioned pine trees align in a magical blue-and-white forest. Intermittent background blocks keep your eye moving across the quilt top for added appeal.

**Quilt is 74" × 80"**

## fabric requirements

**Trees:** 13 assorted blue fat quarters (18" × 22")
**Backgrounds:** 6—½ yard pieces of assorted lights
**Border and Sashing\*:** 1¾ yards total of assorted lights
**Binding:** ⅔ yard of blue fabric
**Backing:** 4¾ yards
**Batting:** 80" × 86"
*\*The featured quilt has a scrappy mix of sashings and borders made with multiple light prints*

## fabric cutting

**Note:** Read assembly directions before cutting. Borders are cut to exact length required plus ¼" seam allowance. WOF designates the width of fabric from selvedge to selvedge (approximately 42" wide).

### Tree Blocks (Darks)

From 13 assorted blue fat quarters, cut:
- 72—Tree A templates (use template on *page 48*)
- 72—1½" × 1½" matching squares for tree trunks

### Backgrounds

From EACH of six light ½ yard pieces, cut:
- 1—11½" × WOF strip
  From those strips, subcut:
  - 1—11½" × 3½" strip (6 total assorted)
  - 3—11½" × 2" strips (18 total assorted)

  Fold the remaining strips in half, right sides together, to cut the tree background templates:
  - 72 matching pairs of background template B and template B reversed (12 pairs from each fabric) (use template on *page 49*)
- 2—1½" × WOF strips
  From those strips, subcut:
  - 144—1½" × 2½" strips (24 from each fabric)

### Borders and Sashing

- 8—3½" × WOF strips
  Sew together strips end to end in pairs, then cut:
  - 2—3½" × 74" side border strips
  - 2—3½" × 74" strips for top and bottom borders
- 10—2" × WOF strips
  Sew the 10 strips end to end to make one long strip. From the long strip, subcut:
  - 5—2" × 68" sashing strips

### Binding:
- 8—2½" × WOF strips

*Use a ¼" seam allowance. Press in the direction of the arrows.*

## construction

1. **Tree block:** Assemble the block as shown using matching Tree A and 1½" × 1½" trunk pieces and matching template B, B reversed, and 2½" × 1½" light pieces. The finished Tree block should measure 5½" × 11½" including seam allowances. Repeat to make 72 Tree blocks total.

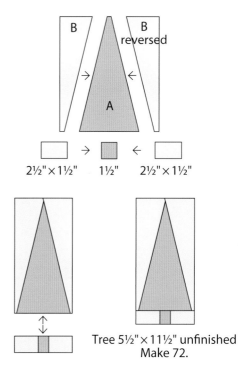

Tree 5½" × 11½" unfinished
Make 72.

## 2 Assemble the rows:

**Row A:** Join 12 Tree blocks, one 3½" × 11½" light strip, and three 2" × 11½" light strips as shown.

**Row B:** Join 12 Tree blocks, one 3½" × 11½" light strip, and three 2" × 11½" light strips as shown.

**Row C:** Join 12 Tree blocks, one 3½" × 11½" light strip, and three 2" × 11½" light strips as shown.

**Row D:** Join 12 Tree blocks, one 3½" × 11½" light strip, and three 2" × 11½" light strips as shown.

**Row E:** Join 12 Tree blocks, one 3½" × 11½" light strip, and three 2" × 11½" light strips as shown.

**Row F:** Join 12 Tree blocks, one 3½" × 11½" light strip, and three 2" × 11½" light strips as shown.

Each row should measure 11½" × 68" including seam allowances.

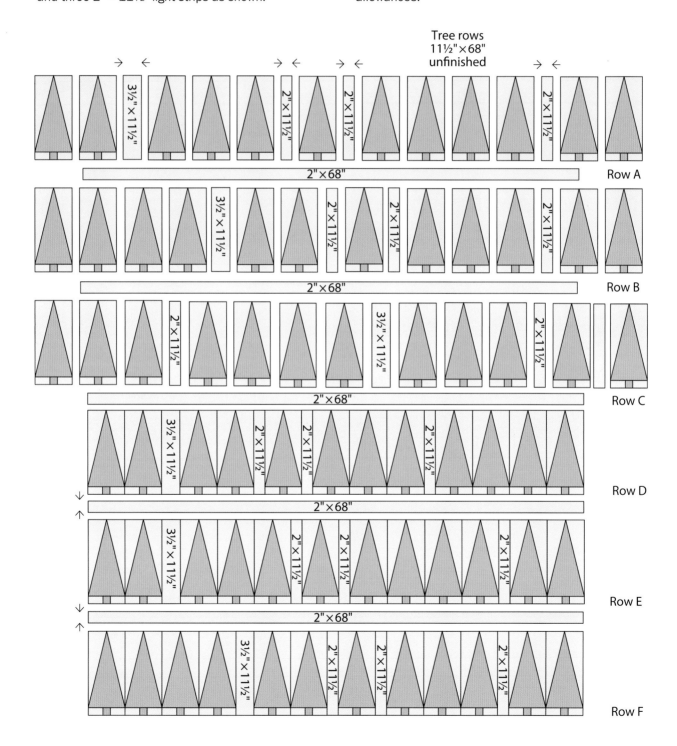

3 Join a 2" × 68" sashing strip to the bottom of each row A–E as shown. Press seam allowances toward the sashing strips. Then join the rows.

4 Add a 3½" × 74" border strip to each quilt side. Then sew 3½" × 74" border strips to the top and bottom edges.

5 **Quilting:** Layer quilt according to the instructions on *page 143*. Quilt as desired.

6 **Binding:** Use the 2½"-wide blue strips to bind the quilt following the instructions on *page 143*.

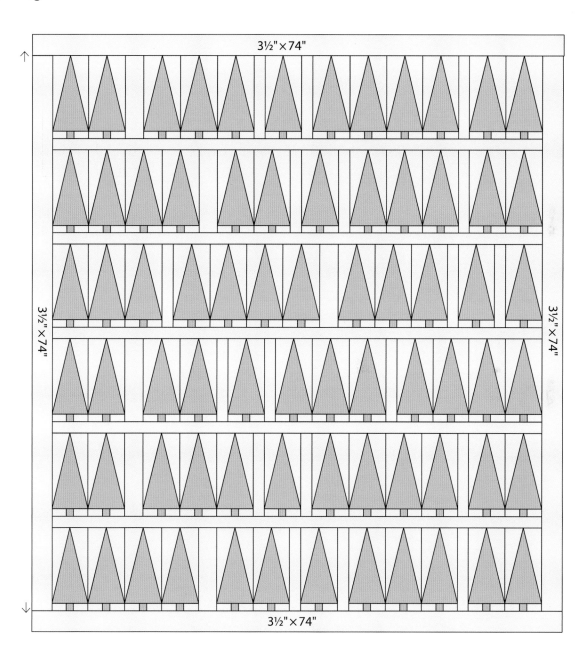

"On a short hike in the mountains around Lake Tahoe I was awed by the amazing pine trees that surround the lake. Nature often inspires my pattern designs." –Edyta

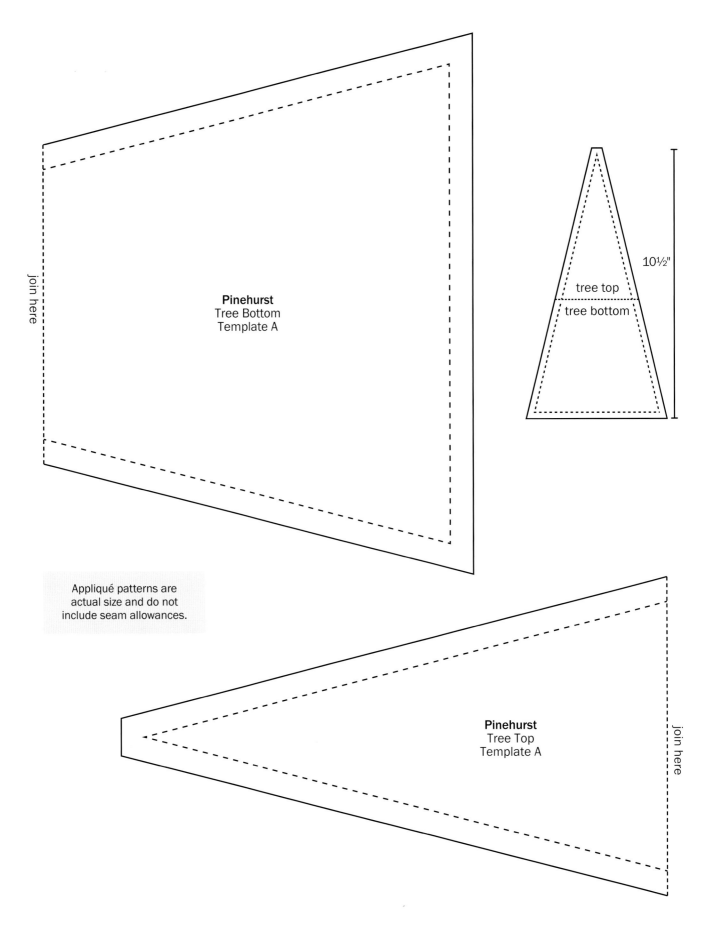

**Pinehurst**
Tree Bottom
Template A

10½"

tree top
tree bottom

join here

Appliqué patterns are
actual size and do not
include seam allowances.

**Pinehurst**
Tree Top
Template A

join here

**Pinehurst**
Tree Background Top
Template B

Cut 72.
Cut 72 reversed.

join here

10½"    top
bottom

join here

**Pinehurst**
Tree
Background
Bottom
Template B

Appliqué patterns are
actual size and do not
include seam allowances.

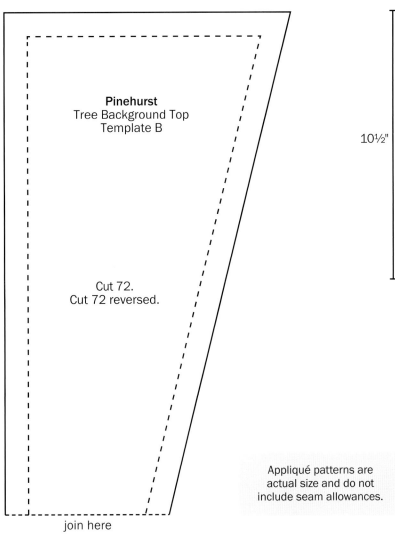

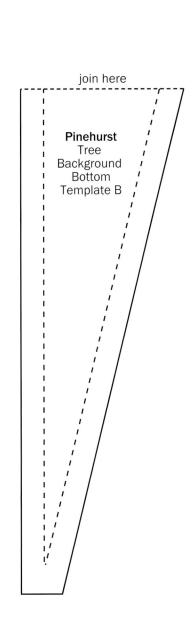

# blooming star

A dimensional "glow" radiates from between each point on beautiful blue stars. Choose your favorite blue star for the center spot and surround it with an appliqué medallion.

**Quilt is 60" × 75"**

# fabric requirements

**Blocks:**
15 blue fat quarters (18" × 21")
6 light fat quarters (18" × 21")
**Block Background:** 2½ yards of light print
**Setting Triangles:** 1 yard of dark cream print
**Appliqué:** 1 package Silhouettes—Perfect Union
(LBQ-0879-S) OR ½ yard of assorted blues
**Inner Border and Binding:** 1 yard of dark blue
**Border:** 1¾ yards of blue floral
**Backing:** 4½ yards
**Batting:** 66" × 81"
**Notions:** spray starch, fabric glue stick

# fabric cutting

**Note:** Pieces for each Star block will be cut one block at a time in Block directions. WOF designates the width of fabric from selvedge to selvedge (approximately 42" wide).

**Block Background:**
- 1—21½" × 21½" square
- 14—11" × 11" squares

**Setting Triangles:**
- 3—16⅛" × 16⅛" squares, cut in half twice diagonally to make ten D quarter-square setting triangles (you will have two leftover triangles)
- 2—8¼" × 8¼" squares, cut once diagonally to make four E half-square triangles

- **Inner Border:**
  8—1½" × WOF strips

- **Border:**
  8—7" × WOF strips

- **Binding:**
  8—2½" × WOF strips

# construction

Visit YouTube.com/LaundryBasketQuilts to view a video tutorial. (Once you're on the Laundry Basket Quilts page, click on "Videos," then search for Episode 25—Shooting Star.)

**Note:** Numbers in parentheses in steps 1–5 reference corresponding photos.

## 1 Block Cutting
(1) For one block you will need the following:
- 1—blue fat quarter
- 1—light fat quarter
- Templates A and B (on page 57)

(2) From the blue fat quarter, cut 12 A pieces.
(3) From your light fat quarter, cut a 2½" × 18" strip.
(4) Using your rotary cutter and Template B, cut 12 triangles from the Step 3 strip as shown.
(5) Each block is created from 12 A and 12 B pieces. The entire quilt is created using 15 stars, each with a different color for A and B pieces.

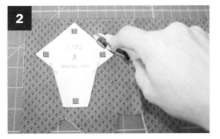

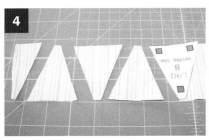

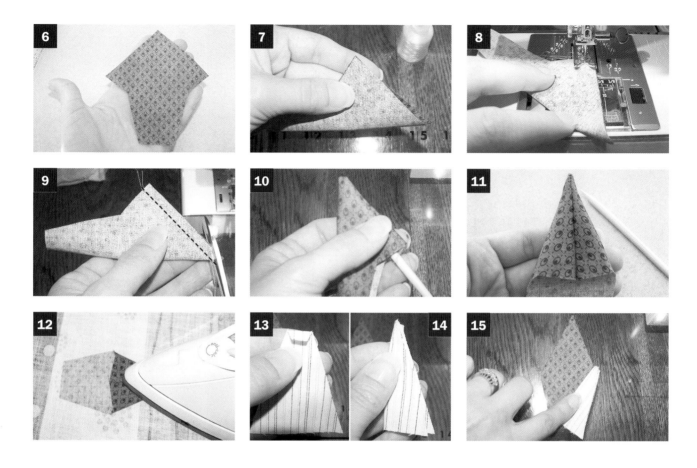

2 **Block Assembly**

    (6) Begin with the blue A piece (blade) right side up in your hand.

(7) Fold the blue A piece in half with right sides together as shown.

(8) Using a ¼" seam allowance, sew from the side point to the tip along the top of the blade.

(9) Trim the inside top tip of your seam allowance, leaving at least a ⅛" seam allowance.

(10) Turn the blade right side out.

(11) Use a chopstick or blunt edge poker to fully turn the point.

(12) Center the seam on the back side of the A piece and press the blade firmly, pushing the seam allowance to one side.

    Repeat for all A pieces. **Note:** Sewing, turning, and pressing the A blades goes very quickly if you're using a chain-piecing technique.

(13) Next take a light B triangle and fold down the tip of it ¼", wrong sides together, as shown; finger-press.

(14) Then with wrong sides together, fold the light B triangle in half lengthwise as shown.

(15) Place the blue A blade right side up, then place the folded light B triangle on the right-hand edge of the A blade.

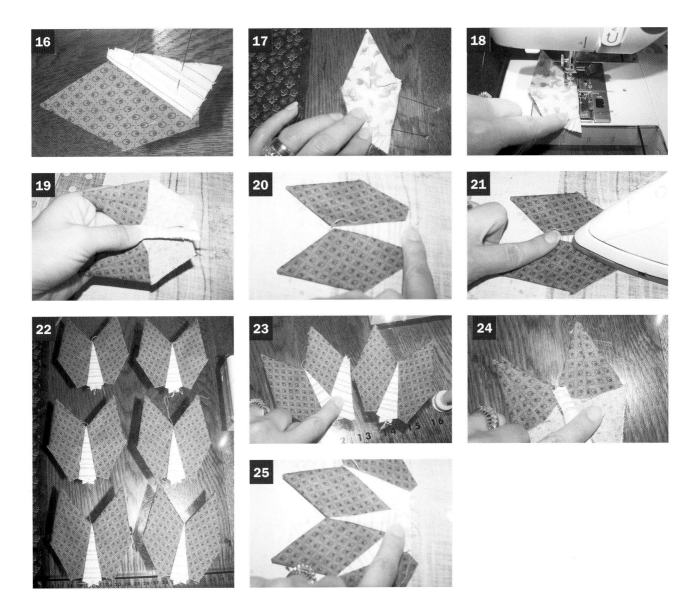

(16) Align all raw edges together and pin as shown.

(17) Lay a second A blade right side down atop the pinned A blade and sandwich the B "glow" between. The light triangle will be wedged between the two A blades.

(18) Beginning with a backstitch to lock your seam, sew through all three pieces using a ¼" seam allowance. Repeat (13)–(18) to make six matching pairs of blue A blades, with a light B triangle insert between them in each seam.

(19) From the wrong side, use your fingers to press the seam allowances open.

(20) Flip the assembly over and place it right side up on an ironing board. Align the light B triangle insert with the center of the seam.

(21) Press the light B triangle down in the center of the seam. Start at the open end of the insert and stop ironing once you are two-thirds of the way to the tip. Use your finger to protect the tip of the light B triangle from being pressed flat.

(22) Repeat (19)–(21) to make and press six blade sets.

(23–24) Sew the blade sets together in the same manner as before, inserting a light B triangle between each pair of A blades.

(25) Press in the same manner as before, following (19)–(21).

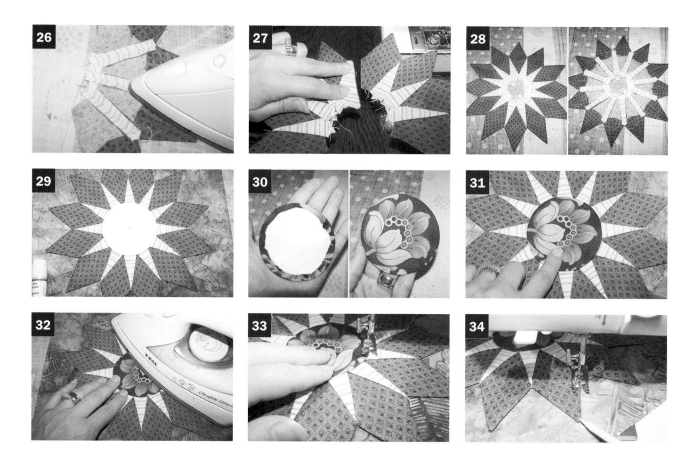

(26) From the wrong side of the pairs, gently press the seam allowances open.

(27) Continue in the same manner until all six pairs of A blades have been joined into a star.

(28) Completed star is shown, front and back.

(29) Press and starch an 11" light background square. Fold the square in half diagonally twice and press to crease with your iron. These pressed lines will establish a center guideline for the star appliqué placement. Using a touch of fabric stick glue on each star point, center it on the background square and adhere it to the background square. Using Template C, cut a circle from freezer paper. Lay this paper circle in the center of your star appliqué making sure that all raw edges in the star center are covered. If it is too big or small, adjust as needed.

(30) Once your freezer-paper template is exactly the size you need, glue the dull side of the freezer paper to the wrong side of your star center blue fabric. Cut out ¼" beyond the outer edge of the freezer paper circle. Turn the raw edges of the fabric circle over to the shiny side of the freezer paper circle and press in place with a warm iron.

(31) Center the circle on the star.

(32) Use your iron and a little glue to attach for easy machine or hand appliqué.

Repeat Step 2 in its entirety to make a total of 15 Star blocks, leaving one star unattached to an 11" background square. It will be used on the center block in Step 4 .

3 **Machine Appliqué**

(33) Use the appliqué method of your choice to stitch the star and center circle to the background square. To use invisible machine appliqué as Edyta does, place a size 90 needle and Wonder Invisible Thread (100% clear nylon) in the top of your machine and cotton thread in a color matching your background fabric in the bobbin. Set your machine's top tension at 0 and use a small zigzag stitch, approximately 20 to 24 stitches per inch.

The zigzag width should be only large enough to grab the background and the appliqué edge. Begin by stitching around the edges of the center circle.

(34) Then stitch around all of the points of the A blades. After your appliqué is sewn to your background square, carefully slit the background fabric under the center circle and remove the freezer paper. Press and starch your block from the wrong side. **Note:** The star and center circle can also be hand appliquéd by using silk thread and a slip stitch if you prefer.

4 **Center Block:** Crease and press the 21½" × 21½" center block background square diagonally twice to locate the center of your block. Place the remaining star in the center of the block aligned as shown below (diagonal lines indicate creases in fabric). Using your preferred method, appliqué the star to the center block.

5 **Appliqué:** Select your favorite appliqué method to add the leaves, berries, and branches from page 58 to the center block as shown.

Appliqué Placement

## 6 Assembling the Quilt Top

Arrange blocks and setting triangles according to the layout below and sew into rows. Sew all rows together. Sew light blue 1½" × WOF inner-border strips end to end in sets of two; press. Sew an inner-border strip to the top and bottom of the quilt center; trim. Then sew inner-border strips to each side; trim excess. Sew blue 7" × WOF border strips end to end in sets of two; press. Sew a border strip to the top and bottom of the quilt center; trim. Then sew a border strip to each remaining side of the quilt center; trim as necessary.

## 7 Quilting:

Layer quilt according to the instructions on page 143. Quilt as desired.

## 8 Binding:

Use the 2½"-wide blue strips to bind the quilt following the instructions on page 143.

**Blooming Star**
Blade
Template A

To create appliqué template from freezer paper for star center, use inner circle. Outer Circle represents a ¼" additional fabric for turn under (seam allowance) on your appliqué.

Lay this paper circle in the center of your appliqué, making sure that all raw edges in the middle are covered. If the circle is too small, enlarge as needed.

**Blooming Star**
Star Center
Template C

**Blooming Star**
Triangle "Glow"
Template B

"Quilts should delight and surprise you. The dimensional light triangles that radiate from the star centers are an unexpected element you might miss until you're up close to the quilt." –Edyta

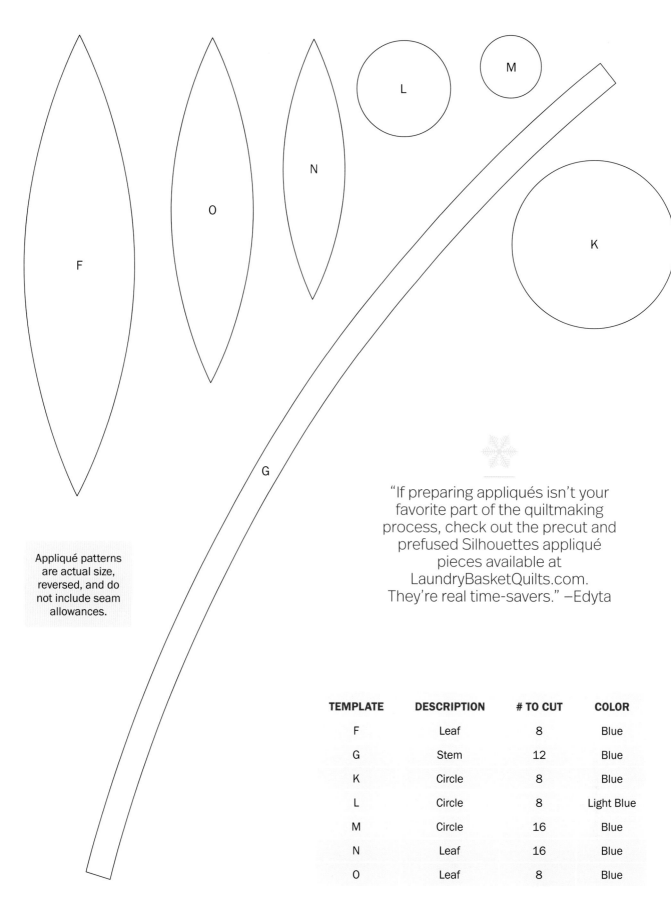

F

O

N

L

M

K

G

Appliqué patterns
are actual size,
reversed, and do
not include seam
allowances.

"If preparing appliqués isn't your
favorite part of the quiltmaking
process, check out the precut and
prefused Silhouettes appliqué
pieces available at
LaundryBasketQuilts.com.
They're real time-savers." –Edyta

| TEMPLATE | DESCRIPTION | # TO CUT | COLOR |
| --- | --- | --- | --- |
| F | Leaf | 8 | Blue |
| G | Stem | 12 | Blue |
| K | Circle | 8 | Blue |
| L | Circle | 8 | Light Blue |
| M | Circle | 16 | Blue |
| N | Leaf | 16 | Blue |
| O | Leaf | 8 | Blue |

# something blue

Add a little sparkle to your decor with light stars shimmering across a sky of assorted blues. Looking for a time-saver? Start with precut 10" squares.

**Quilt is 56½" × 72½"**

# fabric requirements

**Blocks and borders:**
Lights: 27—10" × 10" squares
Blues: 42—10" × 10" squares
**Binding:** ⅔ yard light blue
**Backing:** 3½ yards
**Batting:** 63" × 79"

# fabric cutting

**Note:** Read assembly directions before cutting pieces. Borders are cut to exact length required plus ¼" seam allowance. WOF designates the width of fabric from selvedge to selvedge (approximately 42" wide).

**Light Fabric:**
From 27—10" × 10" squares, cut:
• 12—8½" × 8½" squares for star centers
• 48—4⅞" × 4⅞" squares

**Blue Fabric:**
From 42—10" × 10" squares, cut:
• 48—4⅞" × 4⅞" squares
• 108—4½" × 4½" squares

**Binding**
• 7—2½" × WOF strips

# construction

1 **Block Assembly:**
(A) Place one 4⅞" light square on top of one 4⅞" blue square, right sides together. Draw a diagonal line across the light square. Sew ¼" from each side of the drawn line as shown.

(B) Cut the squares apart on the marked diagonal line to make two half-square triangles. Press the seam allowances toward the blue triangles.

(C) Trim each triangle square to measure 4½" × 4½" to make two of Unit 1. Repeat to make 96 total of Unit 1.

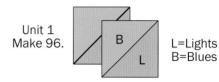

Unit 1
Make 96.

L=Lights
B=Blues

2 Sew together two of Unit 1, noting the position of the blue triangles, to make Unit 2. Repeat to make 48 total of Unit 2.

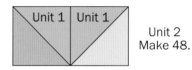

Unit 2
Make 48.

**3** Sew a 4½" blue square to each end of a Unit 2 to make a top row. Repeat to make a bottom row. Sew a Unit 2 to each side of an 8½" light square to make the middle row, again noting the placement of the blue triangles. Sew the rows together to make a Star block, which should be 16½" square including seam allowances. Repeat to make 12 total Star blocks.

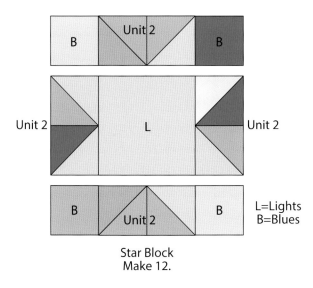

Star Block
Make 12.

**4** Sew together four assorted blue 4½" squares to make a Unit 3 strip. Repeat to make eight Unit 3 strips total.

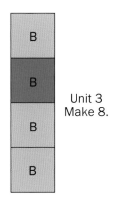

Unit 3
Make 8.

**5** Sew together 14 assorted blue 4½" squares to make a Unit 4 strip. Repeat to make a second Unit 4 strip.

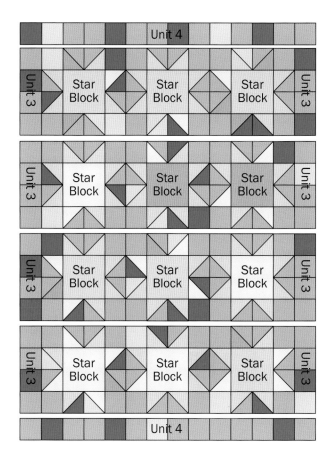

**6** **Quilt-Top Assembly:** Referring to the Quilt Layout above, sew together three Star blocks to make a block row. Sew a Unit 3 strip to each end of the block row to complete. Repeat to make four block rows total.

**7** Join the four Block Rows to make the quilt center. Sew Unit 4 strips to the top and bottom edges of the quilt center to complete the quilt top.

**8** **Quilting:** Layer quilt according to the instructions on page 143. Quilt as desired.

**9** **Binding:** Use the 2½"-wide blue strips to bind the quilt following the instructions on page 143.

Unit 4
Make 2.

| B | B | B | B | B | B | B | B | B | B | B | B | B | B |
|---|---|---|---|---|---|---|---|---|---|---|---|---|---|

# kelley

Collect an assortment of fat quarters in shades of blues as diverse as the sea to make delightfully scrappy Ocean Wave blocks.

**Quilt is 66½" × 81½"**

## fabric requirements

**Blocks/Triangle Squares:**
14—fat quarters (18" × 21") of assorted blues
14—fat quarters (18" × 21") of assorted lights
**Block Background:** 2¼ yards light print
**Border:** 1 yard light floral
**Binding:** ⅔ yard of blue stripe
**Backing:** 5 yards
**Batting:** 73" × 89"
**Optional:** 2 packages 1½"-finished Half-Square Triangle Paper (LBQ–0231)

**Note:** Cutting and Construction are written to use Laundry Basket Quilts Half-Square Triangle Papers (LBQ–0231) for the blocks OR an alternate method. To make half-square triangles with an alternative method, see page 143. WOF designates the width of fabric from selvedge to selvedge (approximately 42" wide).

## fabric cutting

**Assorted Blue** (Half-square triangles)
From the fat quarters cut:
• 40—6" × 21" rectangles to use with LBQ triangle paper (LBQ--0231)
  *OR*
• 80—2⅜" × 21" strips
  From those strips, subcut 640—2⅜" squares

**Assorted Light** (Half-square triangles)
From the fat quarters cut:
• 40—6" × 21" rectangles to use with LBQ triangle paper (LBQ–0231)
  *OR*
• 80—2⅜" × 21" strips
  From those strips, subcut 640—2⅜" squares

**Background Light fabric:**
• 33—2" × WOF strips
  From those strips, subcut:
  • 80—2" × 5" rectangles
  • 160—2" × 3½" rectangles
  • 160—2" squares

**Borders:**
• 8—3½" × WOF strips
  Sew two strips end-to-end to make a long strip.
  Make four long strips. From these long strips, cut:
  • 2—3½" × 75½" side border strips
  • 2—3½" × 66½" top and bottom border strips

**Binding:**
• 8—2½" × WOF strips

*Use ¼" seam allowances. Press in the direction of the arrows.*

## construction

**1** Start with making 1280 (2" unfinished) half-square triangles from assorted blue and light 6" × 21" rectangles. From one sheet of Laundry Basket Quilts 1½"-finished Half-Square Triangle Paper (LBQ--0231), you get 32 half-square triangle units. You will need 40 sheets of paper for this quilt (one package of paper has 25 sheets). (For more details, see page 141.)

**2** Using 16 assorted half-square triangle units from Step 1, two 2" background squares, two 2" × 3½" background rectangles, and one 2" × 5" background rectangle, arrange the pieces in five rows as shown. Sew each row together, then join the rows to make an Ocean Wave unit. The unit should measure 8" square, including seam allowances. Make a total of 80 Ocean Wave units.

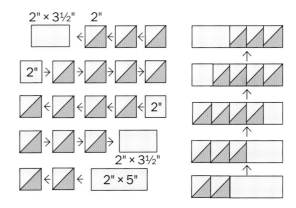

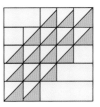

Units
8" × 8" unfinished
Make 80.

$3$ Arrange and sew two rows of two Ocean Wave units as shown. Join the rows to make an Ocean Wave block. The block should measure 15½" square, including seam allowances. Make a total of 20 Ocean Wave blocks.

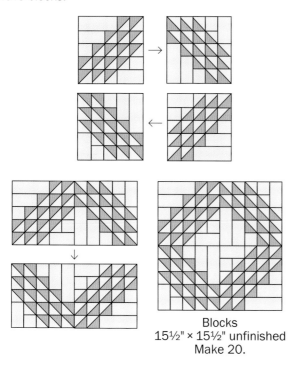

Blocks
15½" × 15½" unfinished
Make 20.

$4$ Arrange and sew five rows of four blocks as shown. Join the rows to make the quilt center.

$5$ Sew the 3½" × 75½" light border strips to the sides of the quilt center. Sew the 3½" × 66½" light borders to the top and bottom.

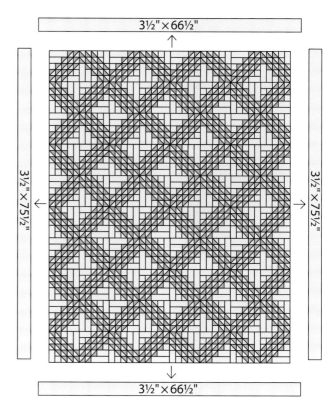

$6$ **Quilting:** Layer quilt according to the instructions on page 143. Quilt as desired.

$7$ **Binding:** Use the 2½"-wide blue strips to bind the quilt following the instructions on page 143.

# winter village

When the first snowflakes fall, nestle under a neighborhood of frosty blue row houses that come together with ease in an eight-block quilt.

**Quilt is 53½" × 66"**

## fabric requirements

**House Windows/Doors (lights):**
8—½ yard pieces of light fabric
4—⅓ yard pieces of light fabric
2—fat eighths (9" × 22") of light fabric

**Houses (darks):**
12—⅔ yard pieces of blue fabric
4—⅓ yard pieces of blue fabric
2—fat quarters (18" × 22") of blue fabric

**Appliqués (darks):**
5—fat eighths (9" × 22") of blue fabric*
4—⅓ yard pieces of blue fabric
2—fat quarters (18" × 22") of blue fabric

**Sashing and Borders (light):**
1¼ yards of light fabric

**Binding:** ⅔ yard of blue fabric

**Batting:** 60" × 72"

**Backing:** 3½ yards

**\*Optional:** 2 packages Laser-Cut Silhouettes
       (LBQ-06380S or LBQ-0726-S)
   1 package Laser-Cut Silhouettes Snowflake
       (LBQ-0393-S)

**Note:** WOF designates the width of fabric from selvedge to selvedge (approximately 42" wide).

## cutting and general construction

1 **Block Cutting and Assembly:** The quilt is made from eight blocks. Each block is made of two or three houses. Block cutting and assembly instructions are listed for each of the eight blocks. Remember to read all instructions for your block before cutting your fabrics. Save all leftovers from blocks as you are creating them. You can use these leftovers in future blocks for a more scrappy look. Press toward darks except when an alternate direction is shown with arrows on the illustration.

2 **Binding:**
From the blue binding fabric, cut:
• 7—2½" × WOF sashing strips

## BLOCK 1: HOUSE 1

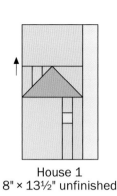

House 1
8" × 13½" unfinished

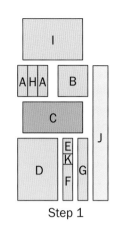

Step 1

**Cutting:**
A: 2 rectangles 1½" × 3½" (light background)
B: 1 square 3½" × 3½" (light background)
C: 1 rectangle 6½" × 3½" (blue roof)
D: 1 rectangle 4½" × 6½" (blue house)
E: 1 rectangle 1½" × 2" (blue house)
F: 1 rectangle 1½" × 4" (blue house)
G: 1 rectangle 1½" × 6½" (blue house)
H: 1 rectangle 1½" × 3½" (blue chimney)
I: 1 rectangle 6½" × 4½" (light background)
J: 1 rectangle 2" × 13½" (light sashing)
K: 1 square 1½" × 1½" (light window)

**Assembly:**
To assemble the roof sew strips A, H, and A together to create a chimney square. After pressing seam allowances towards H, place that unit right sides together with C, making sure the chimney is positioned horizontally. Draw a diagonal line (Step 2), sew on the line, then trim the excess, leaving a ¼" seam allowance. Repeat by placing square B over rectangle C. Press both triangles away from the roof piece after trimming.

   Sew pieces E and F to opposite ends of window K (Step 3). Press seam allowances toward blues. Join D and G pieces to opposite sides of window unit (Step 4). Then join piece I, roof unit, and house.

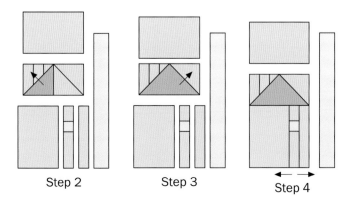

Step 2          Step 3          Step 4

Press in one direction. Sew piece J to right hand side of house unit to complete House 1. The block should measure 11" × 13½" including seam allowances.

## BLOCK 1: HOUSE 2

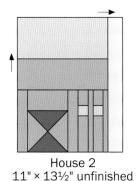

House 2
11" × 13½" unfinished

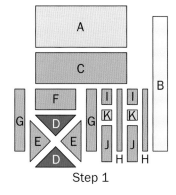

Step 1

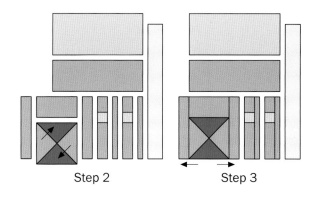

Step 2                 Step 3

## BLOCK 1: HOUSE 3

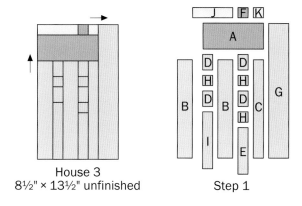

House 3
8½" × 13½" unfinished

Step 1

### Cutting:

A: 1 rectangle 9½" × 4½" (light background)
B: 1 rectangle 2" × 13½" (light sashing)
C: 1 rectangle 9½" × 3½" (blue roof)
D: 1 square 5¼" × 5¼" (blue barn door), cut twice diagonally to make four quarter-square triangles (you'll use two)
E: 1 square 5¼" × 5¼" (blue barn door; different fabric from D), cut twice diagonally to make four quarter-square triangles (you'll use two)
F: 1 rectangle 4½" × 2½" (blue house)
G: 2 rectangles 1½" × 6½" (blue house)
H: 2 rectangles 1" × 6½" (blue house)
I: 2 rectangles 1½" × 2" (blue house)
J: 2 rectangles 1½" × 4" (blue house)
K: 2 squares 1½" × 1½" (light window)

### Assembly:

Sew together D (2 triangles) and E (2 triangles) in two pairs as shown. Then join together pairs to make an hourglass barn door. To press seam allowances in opposite directions at the center, on the back of the block clip and release a few stitches at the center intersection.

Sew pieces I and J to opposite ends of windows K (Step 2). Press toward blues. Add rectangle F to the top of the Hourglass barn door. Join G and H pieces to previously pieced units (Step 3). Continue to add A and C to top of pieced unit to complete House 2, then piece B to the right side of the block. The block should measure 11" × 13½" including seam allowances.

### Cutting :

A: 1 rectangle 3" × 6½" (blue roof)
B: 2 rectangles 2" × 10" (blue house)
C: 1 rectangle 1½" × 10" (blue house)
D: 4 rectangles 1½" × 2" (blue house)
E: 1 rectangle 1½" × 5" (blue house)
F: 1 square 1½" × 1½" (blue chimney)
G: 1 rectangle 2½" × 13½" (light sashing)
H: 3 squares 1½" × 1½" (light window)
I: 1 rectangle 1½" × 6" (light door)
J: 1 rectangle 1½" × 4½" (light background)
K: 1 square 1½" × 1½" (light background)

"I imagine all my friends living in all those cute little houses and we are all quilting neighbors! Enjoy the process of building this little village and choosing prints that reflect your friends' personalities." –Edyta

## Assembly:

As before, sew door (D, H, and I pieces) and window (D, H, and E pieces) units (Step 2). Always press toward the blues. Sew J and K lights to chimney F. Add roof A to chimney unit. Join B and C pieces to the door and window units for the house (Step 3). Sew the roof to the house and the light G piece to the right side of the block to complete House 3. The block should measure 8½" × 13½" including seam allowances.

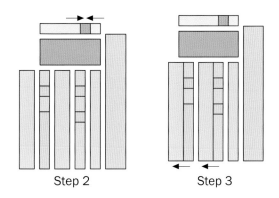

| Step 2 | Step 3 |

## BLOCK 1: ASSEMBLY

Join House 1, House 2, and House 3 in a horizontal row. Press seam allowances in the direction of the arrows. The completed Block 1 should measure 26½" × 13½" including seam allowances.

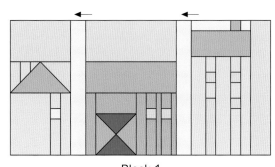

Block 1
26½" × 13½" unfinished

"Like any good construction project, you can't rush the process. Enjoy 'building' your village one house at a time and savor the experience."
—Edyta

## BLOCK 2: HOUSE 4

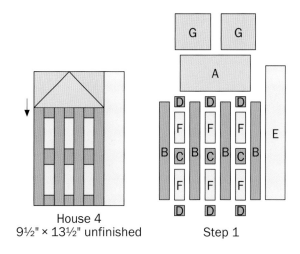

House 4
9½" × 13½" unfinished          Step 1

## Cutting :

A: 1 rectangle 4" × 7½" (blue roof)
B: 4 rectangles 1½" × 10" (blue house)
C: 3 rectangles 1½" × 2" (blue house)
D: 6 squares 1½" × 1½" (blue house)
E: 1 rectangle 2½" × 13½" (light sashing)
F: 6 rectangles 1½" × 3½" (light windows)
G: 2 squares 4" × 4" (light background)

## Assembly:

Assemble the roof by placing square G right sides together on one end of rectangle A. Draw a diagonal line (Step 2), sew on the line, then trim the excess, leaving a ¼" seam allowance. Repeat by placing the remaining square G over rectangle A, trimming and pressing in direction of arrows.

Sew three window unit strips (C, D, and F pieces). Add B pieces between window rows, pressing toward the blues (Step 3). Finish your block by adding the roof to the house and joining piece E to the right side of the house to complete House 4. The block should measure 9½" × 13½" including seam allowances.

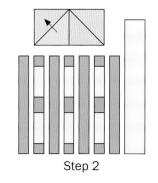 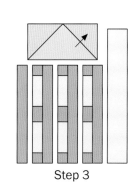

| Step 2 | Step 3 |

# BLOCK 2: HOUSE 5

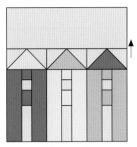

House 5
12½" × 13½" unfinished

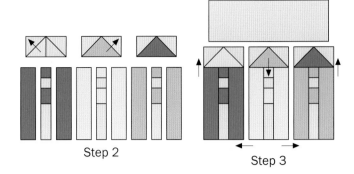

Step 2

Step 3

Finish your block by adding a roof to each house, sewing the houses together, and joining piece G to the top of the roof lines to complete House 5. The block should measure 12½" × 13½" including seam allowances.

## Cutting :

A: 3 rectangles 2½" × 4½" (blue roof)
B: 6 rectangles 2" × 7½" (blue house)
C: 3 squares 1½" × 1½" (blue house)
D: 3 rectangles 1½" × 2" (blue house)
E: 3 squares 1½" × 1½" (light windows)
F: 3 rectangles 1½" × 4" (light door)
G: 1 rectangle 12½" × 4½" (light background)
H: 6 squares 2½" × 2½" (light background)

## BLOCK 2: ASSEMBLY

Sew House 4 and House 5 together. Press seam allowances in the direction of the arrow. The completed Block 2 should measure 21½" × 13½" including seam allowances.

## Assembly:

Comprised of three small town houses, the block starts with making the roofs as you did before. Assemble each roof by placing square H right sides together with on one end of rectangle A. Draw a diagonal line (Step 2), sew on the line, then trim the excess, leaving a ¼" seam allowance. Repeat by placing the remaining square H over rectangle A, trimming and pressing in direction of arrows. Repeat to make three roofs, reversing your pressing direction for the middle roof. (That will help to lock the seams when sewing houses together.)

As before, sew three window and door unit strips (C, D, E, and F pieces). Add B pieces to both sides of each strip to make one townhouse, pressing toward the blues (Step 3). Repeat to make three houses.

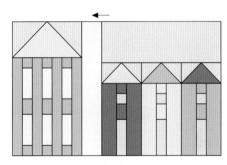

Block 2
21½" × 13½" unfinished

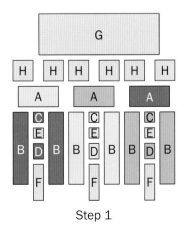

Step 1

## BLOCK 3: HOUSE 6

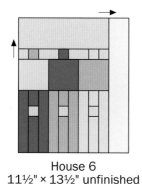

House 6
11½" × 13½" unfinished

**Cutting:**
A: 3 squares 3½" × 3½" (blue roofs)
B: 6 rectangles 1½" × 6½" (blue houses)
C: 3 rectangles 1½" × 4" (blue houses)
D: 3 rectangles 1½" × 2" (blue houses)
E: 3 squares 1½" × 1½" (blue chimneys)
F: 1 rectangle 2½" × 13½" (light sashing)
G: 3 squares 1½" × 1½" (light windows)
H: 1 rectangle 9½" × 3½" (light background)
I: 2 rectangles 1½" × 2½" (light background)
J: 2 squares 1½" × 1½" (light background)

**Assembly:**
Made from 3 small cottages, this block begins by
sewing the chimney row with E, I, and J pieces as shown
(Step 2). Press seam allowance towards chimneys.
Sew a C, D, and G window column together. Press
seams toward the blues. Repeat two more times. Once
completed sew matching B pieces to the left and right
sides of each window column to make three houses.

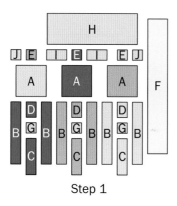

Step 1

Sew three roof A pieces together, positioning them to
match the order of your houses (Step 3). Sew the
chimney row atop the roof piece. Join the three houses,
then sew them to the roof piece. Add the H piece to the
top of the block and the F piece to the right hand side to
complete House 6. The block should measure
11½" × 13½" including seam allowances.

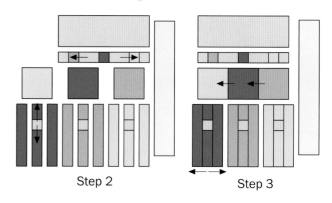

Step 2          Step 3

## BLOCK 3: HOUSE 7

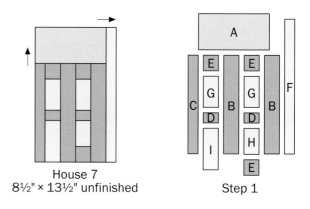

House 7
8½" × 13½" unfinished                Step 1

**Cutting :**
A: 1 rectangle 4" × 7½" (blue roof)
B: 2 rectangles 2" × 10" (blue house)
C: 1 rectangle 1½" × 10" (blue house)
D: 2 rectangles 2" × 1½" (blue house)
E: 3 squares 2" × 2" (blue house)
F: 1 rectangle 1½" × 13½" (light sashing)
G: 2 rectangles 2" × 3½" (light windows)
H: 1 rectangle 2" × 3" (light window)
I: 1 rectangle 2" × 4½" (light door)

The more seams in a block, the more important it is to check that
your ¼" seam allowance is accurate. Doing so will help you finish
blocks at the correct size. Pressing well is also key.

## Assembly:

As before, sew door (D, E, G, and I pieces) and window (D, E, G, and H pieces) units (Step 2). Press seams toward the blues. Sew C and B pieces between the door/window units as shown. Add roof A and sashing F to complete House 7. The block should measure 8½" × 13½" including seam allowances.

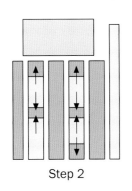

Step 2

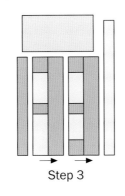

Step 3

## BLOCK 3: HOUSE 8

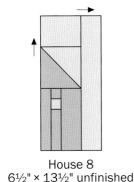

House 8
6½" × 13½" unfinished

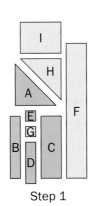

Step 1

### Cutting:

A: 1 square 4⅞" × 4⅞", cut once diagonally to make 2 half-square triangles (you'll use one) (blue roof)

B: 1 rectangle 1½" × 6½" (blue house)

C: 1 rectangle 2½" × 6½" (blue house)

D: 1 rectangle 1½" × 4½" (blue house)

E: 1 square 1½" × 1½" (blue house)

F: 1 rectangle 2½" × 13½" (light sashing)

G: 1 square 1½" × 1½" (light window)

H: 1 square 4⅞" × 4⅞" cut once diagonally to make 2 half square triangles (you'll use one) (light background)

I: 1 rectangle 3½" × 4½" (light background)

## Assembly:

Sew the window column with D, E, and G pieces (Step 2). Press toward the blues. Next, sew half-square triangles A and H together to create a roof (Step 3). Continue to join remaining pieces, first joining the house, then adding the roof, then piece I, and finally piece F to complete House 8. The block should measure 6½" × 13½" including seam allowances.

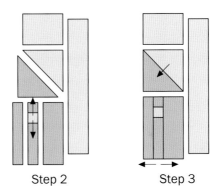

Step 2    Step 3

## BLOCK 3: ASSEMBLY

Join House 6, House 7, and House 8 in a horizontal row. Press seam allowances in the direction of the arrows. The block should measure 25½" × 13½" including seam allowances.

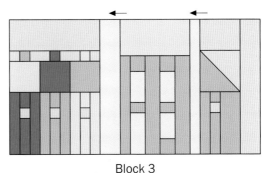

Block 3
25½" × 13½" unfinished

## BLOCK 4: HOUSE 9

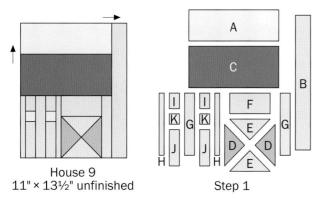

House 9
11" × 13½" unfinished

Step 1

### Cutting:

A: 1 rectangle 9½" × 3½" (light background)
B: 1 rectangle 2" × 13½" (light sashing)
C: 1 rectangle 9½" × 4½" (blue roof)
D: 1 square 5¼" × 5¼" (blue barn door), cut twice diagonally to make 4 quarter-square triangles (you'll use two)
E: 1 square 5¼" × 5¼" (blue barn door; different fabric from piece D), cut twice diagonally to make 4 quarter-square triangles (you'll use two)
F: 1 rectangle 4½" × 2½" (blue house)
G: 2 rectangles 1½" × 6½" (blue house)
H: 2 rectangles 1" × 6½" (blue house)
I: 2 rectangles 1½" × 2" (blue house)
J: 2 rectangles 1½" × 4" (blue house)
K: 2 squares 1½" × 1½" (light window)

### Assembly:

Sew together D (2 triangles) and E (2 triangles) in two pairs as shown (Step 2). Then join together pairs to make an hourglass barn door. To press seam allowances in opposite directions at the center, on the back of the block clip and release a few stitches at the center intersection.

Sew the window columns with I, J, and K pieces, pressing toward the blues. Add piece F to the top of the hourglass barn door. Continue to sew together house pieces as shown (Step 3).

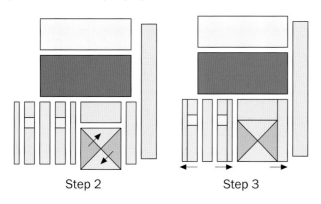

Step 2

Step 3

Connect base of house with C roof, and add G and H pieces to complete House 9. The block should measure 11½" × 13½" including seam allowances.

## BLOCK 4: HOUSE 10

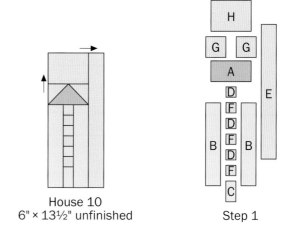

House 10
6" × 13½" unfinished

Step 1

### Cutting:

A: 1 rectangle 4½" × 2½" (blue roof)
B: 2 rectangles 2" × 8½" (blue house)
C: 1 rectangle 1½" × 2½" (blue house)
D: 3 squares 1½" × 1½" (blue house)
E: 1 rectangle 2" × 13½" (light sashing)
F: 3 squares 1½" × 1½" (light window)
G: 2 squares 2½" × 2½" (light background)
H: 1 rectangle 3½" × 4½" (light background)

### Assembly:

Assemble the roof with the A and G pieces as done for House 5 on page 69. Sew the window column with C, D, and F pieces, pressing toward the blues (Step 2). Continue to join remaining pieces, first joining the house, then adding the roof, then piece H, and finally piece E to complete House 10. The finished block should measure 6" × 13½" including seam allowances.

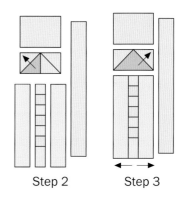

Step 2

Step 3

## BLOCK 4: HOUSE 11

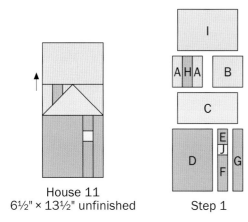

House 11
6½" × 13½" unfinished

Step 1

**Cutting :**
A: 2 rectangles 1½" × 3½" (light background)
B: 1 square 3½" × 3½" (light background)
C: 1 rectangle 6½" × 3½" (blue roof)
D: 1 rectangle 4½" × 6½" (blue house)
E: 1 rectangle 1½" × 2" (blue house)
F: 1 rectangle 1½" × 4" (blue house)
G: 1 rectangle 1½" × 6½" (blue house)
H: 1 rectangle 1½" × 3½" (blue chimney)
I: 1 rectangle 6½" × 4½" (light background)
J: 1 square 1½" × 1½" (light window)

**Assembly:**
Sew the A and H pieces to create a chimney square; press toward the blue. Assemble the roof with the chimney square, B, and C pieces as done for House 1 on page 66, making sure the chimney is positioned horizontally (Step 2).

Sew the window column with E, F, and J pieces, pressing toward the blues (Step 3). In the same manner sew together the base of the house, add the roof, and finally piece I to complete House 11. The block should measure 6½" × 13½" including seam allowances.

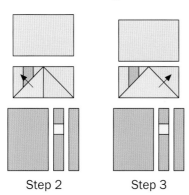

Step 2          Step 3

## BLOCK 4: ASSEMBLY

Sew together House 9, House 10, and House 11 in a horizontal row. Press seam allowances in the direction of the arrows. The block should measure 22½" × 13½" including seam allowances.

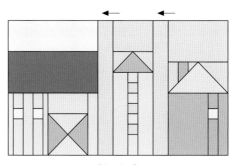

Block 4
22½" × 13½" unfinished

## BLOCK 5: HOUSE 12

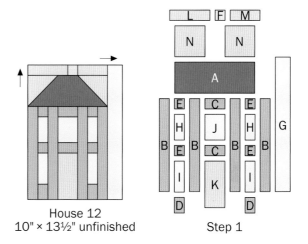

House 12
10" × 13½" unfinished

Step 1

**Cutting:**
A: 1 rectangle 3½" × 8½" (blue roof)
B: 4 rectangles 1½" × 9½" (blue house)
C: 2 rectangles 1½" × 2½" (blue house)
D: 2 rectangles 1½" × 2" (blue house)
E: 4 squares 1½" × 1½" (blue house)
F: 1 square 1½" × 1½" (blue chimney)
G: 1 rectangle 2" × 13½" (light sashing)
H: 2 rectangles 1½" × 3" (light window)
I: 2 rectangles 1½" × 3½" (light window)
J: 1 rectangle 2½" × 3" (light window)
K: 1 rectangle 2½" × 5" (light door)
L: 1 rectangle 1½" × 4½" (light background)
M: 1 rectangle 1½" × 3½" (light background)
N: 2 squares 3½" × 3½" (light background)

**Assembly:**

Referring to Step 2, join pieces L, F, and M to make a chimney strip. In the same manner as the roof of House 10 on page 72, use the A and N pieces to assemble the roof. Make two window columns using the E, D, H, and I pieces. Join the C, J, and K pieces to create the door column. Join the base of the house by sewing together B pieces with the window and door units (Step 3). Add the roof and chimney strip, then the G sashing to complete House 12. The block should measure 10" × 13½" including seam allowances.

**Assembly:**

In the same manner as the roof of House 10 on page 72, use the A and I pieces to assemble the roof (Step 2). Sew two window columns with D, E, and G pieces. Join the B and C pieces as shown to complete the house base (Step 3). Add the roof, H, and F pieces to complete House 13. The block should measure 8" × 13½" including seam allowances.

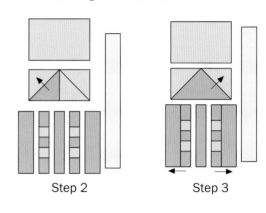

Step 2    Step 3

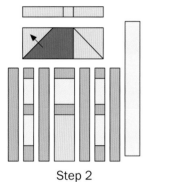
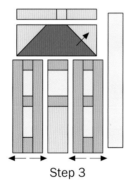

Step 2    Step 3

## BLOCK 5: HOUSE 14

## BLOCK 5: HOUSE 13

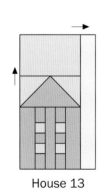
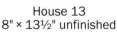

House 13
8" × 13½" unfinished    Step 1

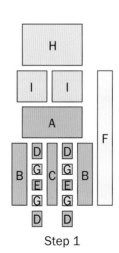

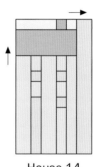
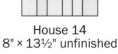
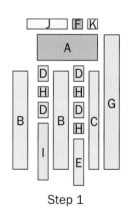

House 14
8" × 13½" unfinished    Step 1

**Cutting:**

A: 1 rectangle 3" × 6½" (blue roof)
B: 2 rectangles 2" × 10" (blue house)
C: 1 rectangle 1½" × 10" (blue house)
D: 4 rectangles 1½" × 2" (blue house)
E: 1 rectangle 1½" × 5" (blue house)
F: 1 square 1½" × 1½" (blue chimney)
G: 1 rectangle 2" × 13½" (light sashing)
H: 3 squares 1½" × 1½" (light window)
I: 1 rectangle 1½" × 6" (light door)
J: 1 rectangle 1½" × 4½" (light background)
K: 1 square 1½" × 1½" (light background)

**Cutting:**

A: 1 rectangle 3½" × 6½" (blue roof)
B: 2 rectangles 2" × 6½" (blue house)
C: 1 rectangle 1½" × 6½" (blue house)
D: 4 rectangles 1½" × 2" (blue house)
E: 2 squares 1½" × 1½" (blue house)
F: 1 rectangle 2" × 13½" (light sashing)
G: 4 squares 1½" × 1½" (light windows)
H: 1 rectangle 6½" × 4½" (light background)
I: 2 squares 3½" × 3½" (light background)

## Assembly:

Sew together D, H, and I pieces to make a door column (Step 2). Join the D, E, and H pieces to make a window column. Sew the F, J, and K pieces together to make a chimney row.

Then sew together the house base, and join the A roof and chimney row. Join the roof to the house, and add the G sashing to complete House 14. The block should measure 8" × 13½" including seam allowances.

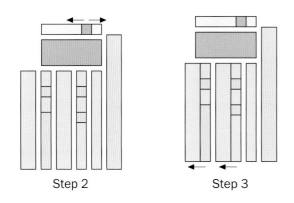

Step 2                     Step 3

## BLOCK 5: ASSEMBLY

Sew together House 12, House 13, and House 14 in a horizontal row. Press seam allowances in the direction of the arrows. The block should measure 25" × 13½" including seam allowances.

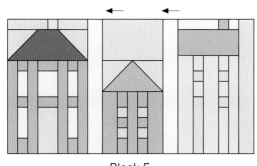

Block 5
25" × 13½" unfinished

"How's your neighborhood coming? Are you moving right along? If I have to get out my seam ripper to fix a block, I tell myself I'm just renovating the house!" –Edyta

## BLOCK 6: HOUSE 15

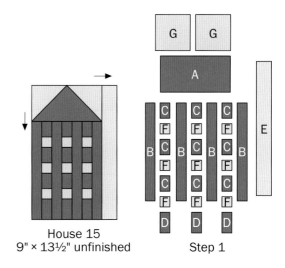

House 15
9" × 13½" unfinished                     Step 1

## Cutting:

A: 1 rectangle 4" × 7½" (blue roof)
B: 4 rectangles 1½" × 10" (blue house)
C: 9 rectangles 1½" × 2" (blue house)
D: 3 rectangles 1½" × 2½" (blue house)
E: 1 rectangle 2" × 13½" (light sashing)
F: 9 squares 1½" × 1½" (light windows)
G: 2 squares 4" × 4" (light background)

## Assembly:

In the same manner as the roof of House 10 on page 72, use the A and G pieces to assemble the roof (Step 2). Join the C, D, and F pieces to make three window columns.

Referring to Step 3, sew together the B pieces and window columns to make the base of the house. Join the roof to the top of the house. Then sew sashing E to complete House 15. The block should measure 9" × 13½" including seam allowances.

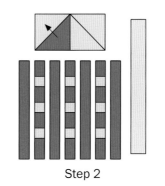
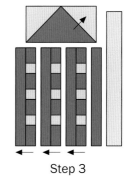

Step 2                     Step 3

# BLOCK 6: HOUSE 16

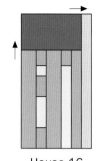

House 16
7½" × 13½" unfinished

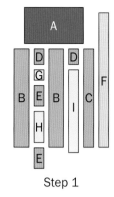

Step 1

**Cutting:**
A: 1 rectangle 4" × 6½" (blue roof)
B: 2 rectangles 2" × 10" (blue house)
C: 1 rectangle 1½" × 10" (blue house)
D: 2 rectangles 1½" × 2" (blue house)
E: 2 rectangles 1½" × 2½" (blue house)
F: 1 rectangle 1½" × 13½" (light sashing)
G: 1 square 1½" × 1½" (light window)
H: 1 rectangle 1½" × 3½" (light window)
I: 1 rectangle 1½" × 8½" (light door)

**Assembly:**
Join the D, E, G, and H pieces to make a window column
(Step 2). Sew together the D and I pieces to make a
door column.

Join those columns with the B and C pieces to form
the base of the house (Step 3). Then join the roof to the
top of the house. Sew the F sashing piece to complete
House 16. The block should measure 7½" × 13½"
including seam allowances.

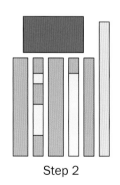

Step 2

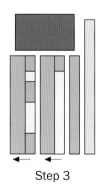

Step 3

# BLOCK 6: HOUSE 17

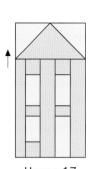

House 17
7½" × 13½" unfinished

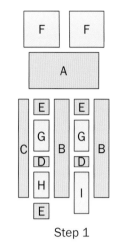

Step 1

**Cutting :**
A: 1 rectangle 4" × 7½" (blue roof)
B: 2 rectangles 2" × 10" (blue house)
C: 1 rectangle 1½" × 10" (blue house)
D: 2 rectangles 1½" × 2" (blue house)
E: 3 squares 2" × 2" (blue house)
F: 2 squares 4" × 4" (light background)
G: 2 rectangles 2" × 3½" (light windows)
H: 1 rectangle 2" × 3" (light window)
I: 1 rectangle 2" × 4½" (light door)

**Assembly:**
In the same manner as the roof of House 10 on
page 72, use the A and F pieces to assemble the roof
(Step 2). Join D, E, G, and H pieces make a window
column. Sew together D, E, G, and I pieces to make a
door column.

Join those columns with the B and C pieces to form
the base of the house (Step 3). Then join the roof
to the top of the house to complete House 17.
The block should measure 7½" × 13½" including
seam allowances.

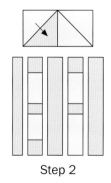

Step 2

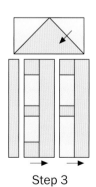

Step 3

## BLOCK 6: ASSEMBLY

Sew together House 15, House 16, and House 17 in a horizontal row. Press seam allowances in the direction of the arrows. The block should measure 23" × 13½" including seam allowances.

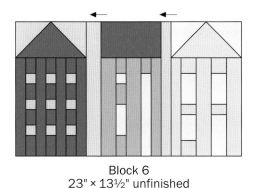

Block 6
23" × 13½" unfinished

## BLOCK 7: HOUSE 18

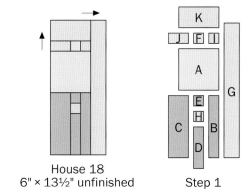

House 18
6" × 13½" unfinished          Step 1

**Cutting:**
A: 1 square 4½" × 4½" (blue roof)
B: 1 rectangle 1½" × 6½" (blue house)
C: 1 rectangle 2½" × 6½" (blue house)
D: 1 rectangle 1½" × 4½" (blue house)
E: 1 square 1½" × 1½" (blue house)
F: 1 square 1½" × 1½" (blue chimney)
G: 1 rectangle 2" × 13½" (light sashing)
H: 1 square 1½" × 1½" (light window)
I : 1 square 1½" × 1½" (light background)
J: 1 rectangle 2½" × 1½" (light background)
K: 1 rectangle 4½" × 2½" (light background)

**Assembly:**
Sew together F, I, and J pieces to make a chimney row (Step 2). Join the D, E, and H pieces to make a window column.

Then sew together the house base and join the A roof to the chimney row. Join the roof to the house, the K sashing to the top, and finally the G sashing to complete House 18. The block should measure 6" × 13½" including seam allowances.

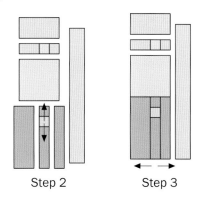

Step 2                    Step 3

## BLOCK 7: HOUSE 19

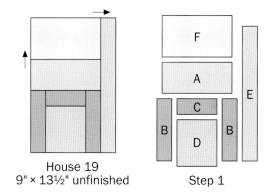

House 19
9" × 13½" unfinished          Step 1

**Cutting:**
A: 1 rectangle 3½" × 7½" (blue roof)
B: 2 rectangles 2" × 6½" (blue house)
C: 1 rectangle 2" × 4½" (blue house)
D: 1 square 4½" × 5" (light door)
E: 1 rectangle 2" × 13½" (light sashing)
F: 1 rectangle 7½" × 4½" (light background)

"My children and my husband are my greatest motivation. Home and family mean everything to me. A house-themed quilt symbolizes where my heart is." –Edyta

**Assembly:**

Sew together pieces C and D to make the door unit (Step 2). Add B pieces on opposite sides of the door unit to make the house base. Then add roof A to the house unit (Step 3). Finish your block by first adding piece F and then piece E to complete House 19. The block should measure 9" × 13½" including seam allowances.

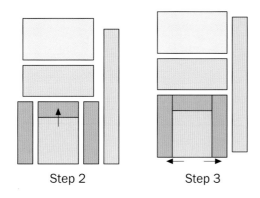

Step 2          Step 3

## BLOCK 7: HOUSE 20

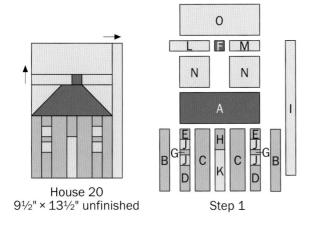

House 20
9½" × 13½" unfinished          Step 1

**Cutting :**

A: 1 rectangle 3½" × 8½" (blue roof)
B: 2 rectangles 1½" × 6½" (blue house)
C: 2 rectangles 2" × 6½" (blue house)
D: 2 rectangles 1½" × 3" (blue house)
E: 2 squares 1½" × 1½" (blue house)
F: 1 square 1½" × 1½" (blue chimney)
G: 2 rectangles 1½" × 1" (blue house)
H: 1 rectangle 1½" × 2½" (blue house)
I: 1 rectangle 1½" × 13½" (light sashing)
J: 4 squares 1½" × 1½" (light window)
K: 1 rectangle 1½" × 4½" (light door)
L: 1 rectangle 1½" × 4½" (light background)
M: 1 rectangle 1½" × 3½" (light background)
N: 2 squares 3½" × 3½" (light background)
O: 1 rectangle 8½" × 3½" (light background)

**Assembly:**

Sew together F, L, and M pieces to make a chimney row (Step 2). In the same manner as the roof of House 10 on page 72, use the A and N pieces to assemble the roof. Join the D, E, G, and J pieces to make a pair of window columns (Step 2). Sew together the H and K pieces to make a door column. Then sew together the house base with B and C pieces and the door and window units to make the house base (Step 3). Join the roof, chimney row, and piece O. Then join the roof unit and house base. Finally, add the I sashing to complete House 20. The block should measure 9½" × 13½" including seam allowances.

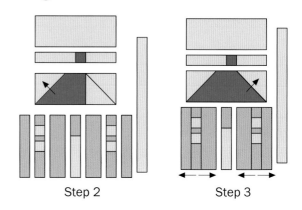

Step 2          Step 3

## BLOCK 7: ASSEMBLY

Sew together House 18, House 19, and House 20 in a horizontal row. Press seam allowances in the direction of the arrows. The block should measure 23½" × 13½" including seam allowances.

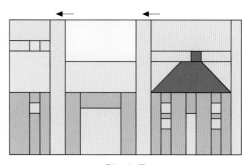

Block 7
23½" × 13½" unfinished

## BLOCK 8: HOUSE 21

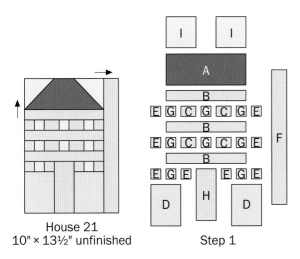

House 21
10" × 13½" unfinished

Step 1

**Cutting:**

A: 1 rectangle 3½" × 8½" (blue roof)

B: 3 rectangles 1½" × 8½" (blue house)

C: 4 rectangles 1½" × 2" (blue house)

D: 2 rectangles 3½" × 4½" (blue house)

E: 8 squares 1½" × 1½" (blue house)

F: 1 rectangle 2" × 13½" (light sashing)

G: 8 squares 1½" × 1½" (light window)

H: 1 rectangle 2½" × 5½" (light door)

I: 2 squares 3½" × 3½" (light background)

**Assembly:**

In the same manner as the roof of House 10 on page 72, use the A and I pieces to assemble the roof (Step 2). Join C, E, and G pieces make to make two long window rows. Sew together E and G pieces to make two short window segments.

Sew the short window segments to the top of the D pieces (Step 3). Join these two units on either side of the H door for the base of house. Sew the roof, B pieces, window rows, and house base together. Finally, add the F sashing to complete House 21. The block should measure 10" × 13½" including seam allowances.

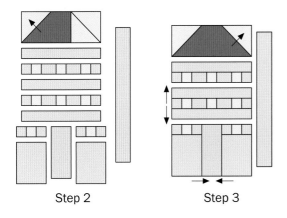

Step 2

Step 3

## BLOCK 8: HOUSE 22

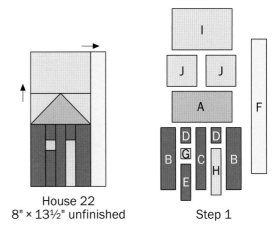

House 22
8" × 13½" unfinished

Step 1

**Cutting:**

A: 1 rectangle 3½" × 6½" (blue roof)

B: 2 rectangles 2" × 6½" (blue house)

C: 1 rectangle 1½" × 6½" (blue house)

D: 2 rectangles 1½" × 2" (blue house)

E: 1 rectangle 1½" × 4" (blue house)

F: 1 rectangle 2" × 13½" (light sashing)

G: 1 square 1½" × 1½" (light window)

H: 1 rectangle 1½" × 5" (light door)

I: 1 rectangle 6½" × 4½" (light background)

J: 2 squares 3½" × 3½" (light background)

**Assembly:**

In the same manner as the roof of House 10 on page 72, use the A and J pieces to assemble the roof (Step 2). Join D, E, and G pieces make to a window column. Sew together D and H pieces to make a door column. Join those columns with B and C pieces to form the base of the house (Step 3).

Then join the roof and I piece to the top of the house. Finish by adding F sashing to complete House 22. The block should measure 8" × 13½" including seam allowances.

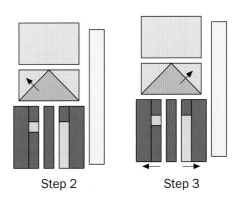

Step 2

Step 3

## BLOCK 8: HOUSE 23

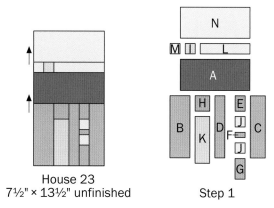

House 23
7½" × 13½" unfinished

Step 1

**Cutting:**

A: 1 rectangle 3½" × 7½" (blue roof)
B: 1 rectangle 2½" × 6½" (blue house)
C: 1 rectangle 2" × 6½" (blue house)
D: 1 rectangle 1½" × 6½" (blue house)
E: 1 rectangle 1½" × 2" (blue house)
F: 1 rectangle 1½" × 1" (blue house)
G: 1 rectangle 1½" × 2½" (blue house)
H: 1 square 2" × 2" (blue house)
I: 1 square 1½" × 1½" (blue chimney)
J: 2 squares 1½" × 1½" (light window)
K: 1 rectangle 2" × 5" (light door)
L: 1 rectangle 1½" × 5½" (light background)
M: 1 square 1½" × 1½" (light background)
N: 1 rectangle 7½" × 3½" (light background)

**Assembly:**

Sew together I, L, and M pieces to make a chimney row (Step 2). Join the H and K pieces to make a door column. Sew the E, F, G, and J pieces together to make a window column.

Join those columns with B, C, and D pieces to form the base of the house (Step 3). Sew the roof, chimney row, and N piece together, then join that piece to the house base to complete House 23. The block should measure 7½" × 13½" including seam allowances.

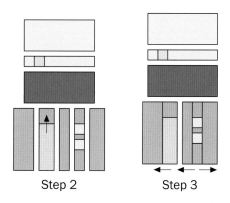

Step 2

Step 3

## BLOCK 8: ASSEMBLY

Sew together House 21, House 22, and House 23 in a horizontal row. Press seam allowances in the direction of the arrows. The block should measure 24½" × 13½" including seam allowances.

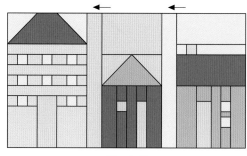

Block 8
24½" × 13½" unfinished

## completing the quilt

1 **Quilt-Top Assembly:** Once all blocks are completed, arrange the eight blocks in four rows as shown on page 81. Sew the blocks together in pairs to make four rows; press all seam allowances in the direction shown.

From the sashing and border fabric, cut:
- 6—3½" × WOF border strips
  Sew those strips end to end. From this long strip cut two 3½" × 66" long border strips and two 3½" × 47½" top and bottom border strips.
- 4—3" × WOF sashing strips
  Sew those strips end to end. From this long strip cut three 3" × 47½" sashing strips.

Consider personalizing
your quilt by stitching your
last name and the year
your family was established
along a border, or by adding
a few embroidered details
to the houses.

Sew a 3" × 47½" sashing strip to each bottom edge of the first three rows. Using pins to ensure accuracy, join all rows to make the quilt center. Finish the pieced quilt by adding 3½" × 47½" borders to top and bottom, then sewing the 3½" × 66" border strips to each side as shown below. Press all seam allowances toward the borders. Prepare your quilt to add appliqué.

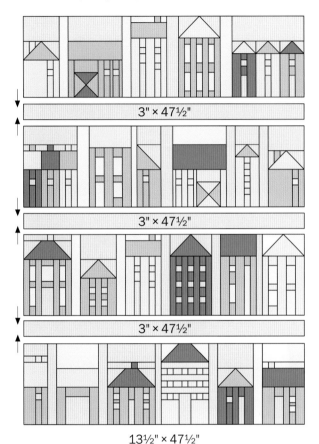

3" × 47½"

3" × 47½"

3" × 47½"

13½" × 47½"

3½" × 47½"

3½" × 66"

3½" × 66"

3½" × 47½"

2 **Appliqué:** Choose your favorite appliqué method to appliqué the branches, birds, berries, and snowflakes around the border, referring to the photograph for placement. (See Appliqué options beginning on page 138.) I used Silhouettes for the appliqué of the featured quilt.

3 **Quilting:** Layer the quilt according to the instructions on page 143. Quilt as desired.

4 **Binding:** Use the 2½"-wide blue strips to bind the quilt following the instructions on page 143.

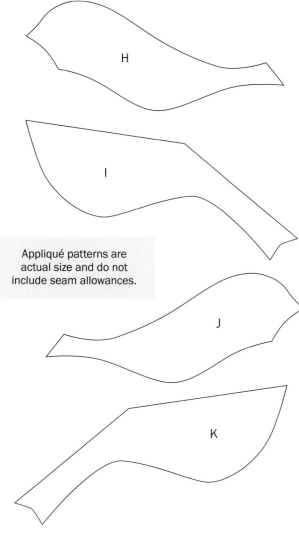

H

I

Appliqué patterns are
actual size and do not
include seam allowances.

J

K

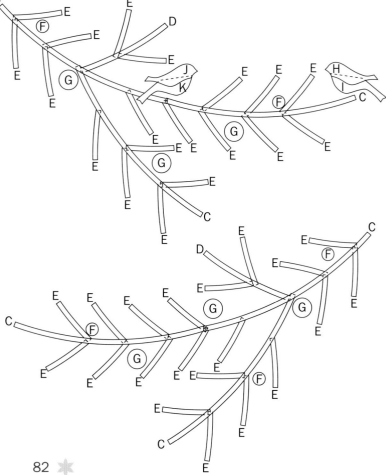

| TEMPLATE | DESCRIPTION | # TO CUT |
| --- | --- | --- |
| A | Snowflake Small | 3 blue |
| B | Snowflake Large | 3 blue |
| C | Stem Large | 12 blue |
| D | Stem Medium | 4 blue |
| E | Stem Small | 78 blue |
| F | Circle Small | 10 blue |
| G | Circle Large | 12 blue |
| H | Body R | 2 blue |
| I | Bird R | 2 blue |
| J | Body L | 2 blue |
| L | Bird L | 2 blue |

Appliqué patterns are actual size, reversed, and do not include seam allowances.

83

# crystal ball

To piece or not to piece isn't the question. To piece or appliqué is!
Which technique will you choose to create a twirling,
swirling eye-catching quilt?

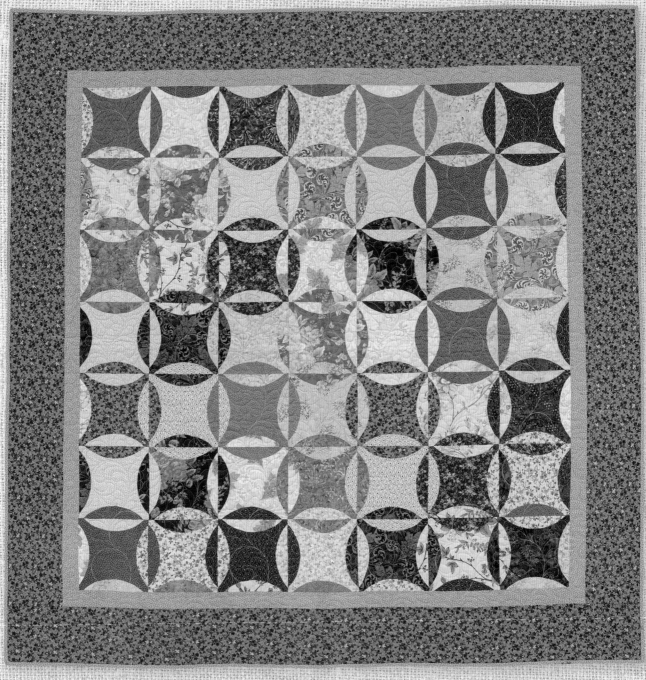

**Quilt is 59" × 59"**

## fabric requirements

**Blocks:**
  25—fat eighths (9" × 21") of assorted blues
  24—fat eighths (9" × 21") of assorted lights
**Inner Border and Binding:** 1 yard of tan print
**Outer Border:** 1 yard of blue
**Backing:** 3¾ yards
**Batting:** 65" × 65"

## fabric cutting

**Note:** Read assembly directions before cutting pieces. Borders are cut to exact length required plus ¼" seam allowance. WOF designates the width of fabric from selvedge to selvedge (approximately 42" wide).

**Inner Borders and Binding:**
• 7—2½" × WOF strips for binding
• 5—2" × WOF strips for inner borders. Sew those strips end-to-end to make a long strip.
  From that long strip, cut:
  • 2—2" × 46" side border strips
  • 2—2" × 49" top and bottom border strips

**Borders:**
• 6—5½" × WOF strips
  Sew three strips end-to-end to make a long strip. Make two long strips. From those long strips, cut:
  • 2—5½" × 49" side border strips
  • 2—5½" × 59" top and bottom border strips

## construction

There are two different techniques that may be used to complete this quilt. Technique 1: Traditional Piecing using templates and Technique 2: Appliqué. Please read through all directions before starting and choose your preferred technique. Numbers in (parenthesis) refer to a corresponding photo.

1 **Technique 1: Traditional Piecing**
  (1) Press the fat eighths and layer them one on top of the other with right sides up. (I like to cut through three layers at a time).
  (2) Using a rotary cutter and a ruler, precut each fat eighth into the following: one 7" square and four 7" × 1¾" strips. Keep the fabric stacked after it is cut as shown. Cut 49 sets of 1 square and 4 strips.
  (3) Using the templates on pages 88 and 89, cut one A piece from each 7" square. Cut four B pieces, one each from the 7 × 1¾" strips cut in (2).
  (4) You should have one set of an A piece and four matching B pieces from each fat eighth. Repeat cutting until you have 49 matching sets.
  (5) Begin laying out your A pieces in seven rows, each seven blocks wide, beginning with a dark A piece and alternating lights and darks. Keep the four matching B pieces atop each A piece for now to keep the colors organized.
  (6) Once you are pleased with your color placement, position the B pieces into the neighboring blocks, filling up the cut-out arcs as shown. The last rectangle arc in a row or column should be switched with the first rectangle arch in that row or column. (See the diagram on page 88 for an illustration.)

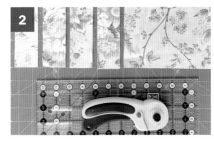
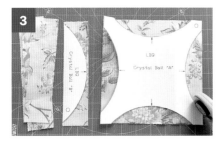
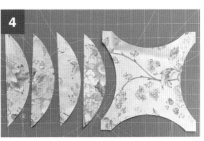

(7) To assemble the blocks, begin with an A piece right side up on your sewing-machine bed. Place the adjacent B arc face down with the curve of the arc touching at the center of the A piece where it aligns.

(8) Match the centers of the A and B pieces and place a pin in the middle of the arc to secure it as shown. After pieces are pinned, flip unit over so the A piece is on top of the B piece. You are ready to sew.

(9) Using a universal needle, cotton thread in your sewing machine, and a stitch length of 2 (smaller stitch length will make turning easier), proceed to sew the curved pieces together. Notice that the bunny ear from the B piece needs to be sticking out to approximately ¼" for the seam allowance. Keeping the A piece atop the B piece will make it easier to sew the curve.

(10) Starting at the edge of the A arc, sew 2–3 stitches then stop. Align the edges of A and B as shown and sew to the center pin.

(11) Stop at the pin with your needle position down, remove the pin, and align the remaining edges of the A and B arcs, making sure that a ¼" bunny ear is sticking out at the end of arc. Finish sewing to the end.

(12) In the same manner, repeat (7)–(11) for the three remaining arcs of the block.

Once all of the blocks are completed, arrange them in seven rows of seven blocks each; sew the blocks into rows then sew the rows together (see the assembly diagram on page 88). Press the seam allowances in opposite directions or open to create a smooth transition of nested seams throughout the quilt top.

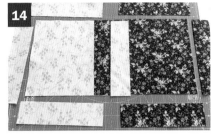

## 2 Technique 2: Appliqué

(13) Press the fat eighths. Using a rotary cutter and a ruler, precut each fat eighth into the following: one 7" square and four 7" × 1¾" strips. Keep the fabric stacked after it is cut as shown. Cut 49 sets of one square and four strips.

(14) Begin laying out your A pieces into seven rows, each seven blocks wide, beginning with a dark A piece and alternating lights and darks. Keep the four matching B pieces atop each A piece for now to keep the colors organized. Once you're satisfied with the color placement, place the four matching rectangles on each side of the matching A squares as shown.

(15) Pair a 7" × 1¾" rectangle with a 7" × 1¾" rectangle of the adjacent block, then sew together along one long edge as shown. Press seam allowances open. Repeat to sew all the rectangle pairs together, returning them to their correct position in your layout as you go. (**Note:** On the outer edges of quilt, leave the single rectangles to cut the shapes from later.)

In the same manner, sew the 7" squares together into rows of seven blocks each and then sew rows together into a quilt top, again making sure you keep A blocks in the same positions as your layout.

(16) Press all seam allowances open.

(17) Use Template C and your favorite technique to prepare the appliqués. I used machine appliqué. Trace the C shape onto freezer paper, press it to the wrong side of the two rectangles sewn together, cut the fabric a ¼" bigger around than the freezer paper shape, and then turn the edges onto the freezer paper, starting with the tips as shown. (**Note:** On the outer edges of the quilt, use Template B and a single rectangle for the shape, cutting at least ¼" around all edges.)

(18) Place the appliqué on the seam between two A (related color) squares and appliqué the piece in place. I use a Microtex needle size 70/10, nylon invisible thread in the needle, cotton thread in the bobbin, and set my machine top tension to zero. Using a small zigzag stitch, attach the C appliqué piece to the quilt top, centering it and aligning the seamlines. Repeat to appliqué all C pieces in place.

Once all the pieces are appliquéd to the quilt top, carefully cut the fabric from the back of the quilt behind each appliqué to remove the freezer paper.

"Some quilters skip over patterns with curves, thinking they're too difficult. But having the option to piece OR appliqué them lets you choose the method that's easier for you." –Edyta

# complete the quilt

3 **Inner Border:** Sew a 2" × 45½" inner-border strip to opposite quilt sides. Press toward the border. Add the 2" × 48" inner-border strips to the remaining edges.

4 **Outer Border:** Sew a 5½" × 48" outer-border strip to opposite quilt sides. Press toward the border. Add the 5½" × 58½" outer-border strips to the remaining edges.

5 **Quilting:** Layer quilt according to the instructions on page 143. Quilt as desired.

6 **Binding:** Use the 2½"-wide tan print strips to bind the quilt following the instructions on page 143.

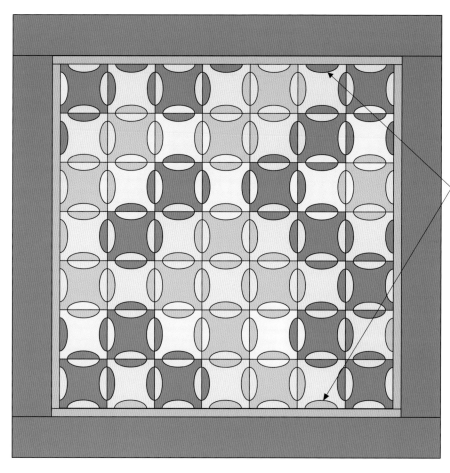

Switch rectangle arches at the ends of all rows and columns when you lay out your quilt.

Seam allowance is included in template size.

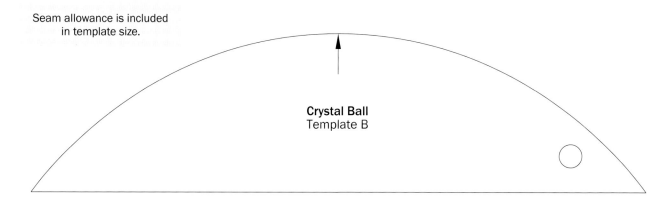

**Crystal Ball**
Template B

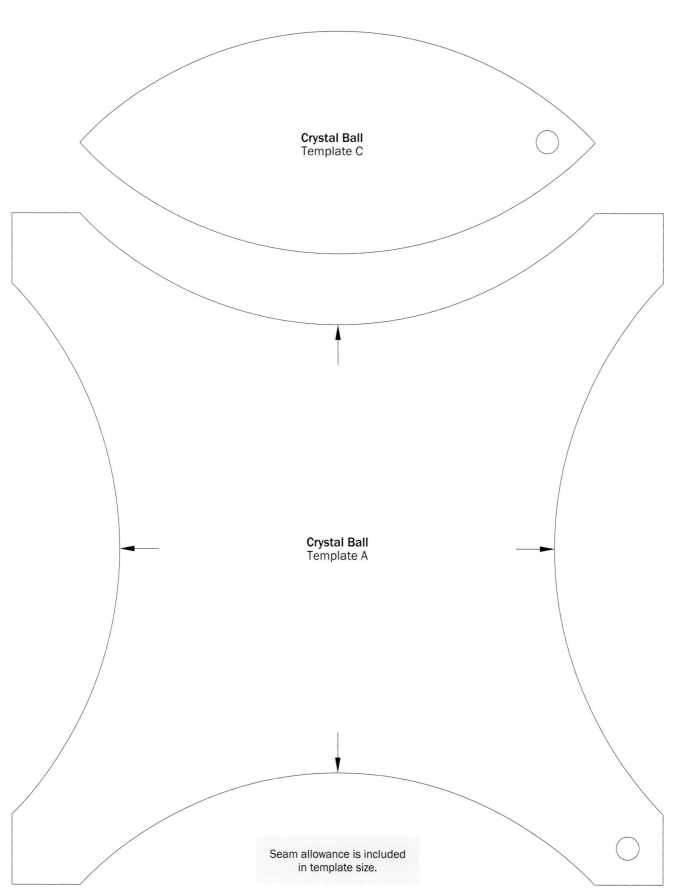

**Crystal Ball**
Template C

**Crystal Ball**
Template A

Seam allowance is included
in template size.

# aspen

There might be frost on the windowpanes,
but you'll be chasing off the winter chill curled up
in a one-of-a-kind snowflake throw.

**Quilt is 88½" × 88½"**

# fabric requirements

### Blocks and Border:
12—fat eighths (9" × 22") of blue fabrics (snowflake)*
4—¼ yard pieces of blue fabrics (snowflake)*
8½ yards of light fabric (background and border)
**Binding:** ¾ yard of blue fabric
**Backing:** 8 yards of blue fabric
**Batting:** 95" × 95"
* To replicate shading, balance fabric selection with mix of lights, mediums, and darks

# fabric cutting

**\*\*Note:** When cutting the blues, separate them into lights, mediums, and darks. When making units, pay close attention to where units will be positioned to give the shading of dark to light from the center of the quilt outward. Be flexible, but try to keep the shading of the colors as a priority when positioning units. Please read through all instructions before starting. WOF designates the width of fabric from selvedge to selvedge (approximately 42" wide).

### Blue Fabric:
From EACH of 12 blue fat eighths, cut:
• 5—1½" × 20" fabric strips

From the four blue ¼ yards, cut\*\*:
• 1—5½" × 20" strip
• 1—2½" × 20" fabric strip
• 10—1½" × WOF strips
  From 8 of those strips, subcut:
  • 4 —1½" × 36½" sashing strips
  • 8—1½" × 12½" sashing strips
  • 8—1½" × 4½" sashing strips
  • 4—1½" × 3½" sashing strips
  • 4— 1½" × 1½" squares
  From remaining two strips, subcut:
  • 8—1½" × 4½" rectangles
  • 8—1½" × 2½" rectangles
  • 8—1½" × 1½" squares

### Light Backgrounds:
• 6—9½" × WOF light strips
  From those strips, subcut:
  • 4—9½" × 26½" strips
  • 4—9½" × 17½" rectangles

• 2—5½" × WOF light strips
  From those strips, subcut:
  • 8—5½" × 5½" squares

• 7—4½" × WOF light strips
  From those strips, subcut:
  • 8—4½" × 17½" background rectangles
  • 8—4½" × 9½" background rectangles
  • 8—4½" × 4½" background squares

• 8—3½" × WOF light strips
  From those strips, subcut:
  • 8—3½" × 7½" background rectangles
  • 8—3½" × 6½" background rectangles
  • 24—3½" × 4½" background rectangles
  • 16—3½" × 3½" background squares

• 27—2½" × WOF light strips
  From those strips, subcut:
  • 13—2½" × 20" strips
  • 8—2½" × 12½" background rectangles
  • 8—2½" × 10½" background rectangles
  • 8—2½" × 8½" background rectangles
  • 16—2½" × 6½" background rectangles
  • 8—2½" × 5½" background rectangles
  • 72—2½" × 3½" background rectangles
  • 32—2½" × 2½" background squares

• 40—1½" × WOF light strips
  From those strips, subcut:
  • 58—1½" × 20" strips
  • 8—1½" × 7½" background rectangles
  • 8—1½" × 5½" background rectangles
  • 40—1½" × 3½" background rectangles
  • 48—1½" × 2½" background rectangles
  • 20— 1½" × 1½" background squares

### Border:
• 9—2" × WOF light strips
  Sew strips together end to end, then subcut:
  • 2—2" × 88½" border strips
  • 2—2" × 85½" border strips

### Binding:
10—2½" × WOF blue strips

# construction

*Use a ¼" seam allowance. Press in the direction of the arrows or press seam allowances open.*

## 1 Assembly of Units & Patches

(A) Sew together one light and two blue 1½" × 20" strips to make an A strip set. Press toward the blue strips. Make four A strip sets total. Cut 12—1½"-wide segments (Unit A) from each strip set (48 total). Set aside 16 Unit A segments.

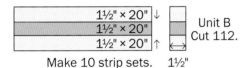

Make 4 strip sets.

(B) Sew together one blue and two light 1½" × 20" strips to make a B strip set. Make 10 B strip sets total. Cut 12—1½"-wide segments (Unit B) from each strip set (112 total). Set aside 24 Unit B segments.

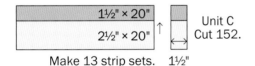

Make 10 strip sets.

(C) Sew together one light 2½" × 20" strip and one blue 1½" × 20" strip to make a C strip set. Make 13 C strip sets. Cut 12—1½" wide segments from each strip set (152 total). Set aside eight Unit C segments.

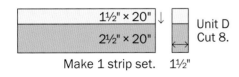

Make 13 strip sets.

(D) Sew together a light 1½" × 20" strip and a blue 2½" × 20" strip to make a D strip set. Cut 8—1½" wide Unit D segments from the strip set.

Make 1 strip set.

(E) Join two Unit A segments and one Unit B segment as shown to make a Nine Patch block. Repeat to make 12 total.

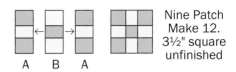

Nine Patch Make 12. 3½" square unfinished

(F) Join two Unit C segments and one Unit B segment as shown to make a Seven Patch block. Repeat to make 68 total.

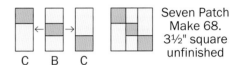

Seven Patch Make 68. 3½" square unfinished

(G) Join one Unit A , one Unit B, and one Unit C segment as shown to make an Eight Patch block. Repeat to make eight total.

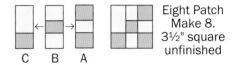

Eight Patch Make 8. 3½" square unfinished

(H) Sew one blue and two light 1½" × 20" strips together to make a strip set. Repeat to make three strip sets total. From strip sets, cut:
- 4—3½" × 6½" units
- 4—3½" × 4½" units
- 4—3½" × 2½" units

Make 3 strip sets.

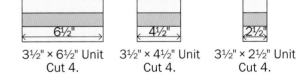

3½" × 6½" Unit Cut 4.     3½" × 4½" Unit Cut 4.     3½" × 2½" Unit Cut 4.

## 2 Assembly of Four Patch blocks & Units

(A) Sew together a light 1½" × 20" strip and a blue 1½" × 20" strip to make an E strip set. Press toward the blue strip. Make 20 E strip sets total. Cut 12—1½" wide segments (Unit E) from each strip set (236 total). Set aside 32 Unit E segments.

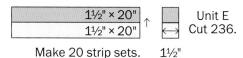

Make 20 strip sets.  Unit E Cut 236.  1½"

(B) From the remaining Unit E segments, join two E segments as shown to make a Four Patch. Repeat to make 102 Four Patches total.

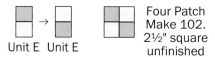

Unit E  Unit E

Four Patch
Make 102.
2½" square
unfinished

## 3 Strip Units

(A) Sew together one light 1½" × 20" strip and one blue 1½" × 20" strip to make a strip set. Repeat to make five strip sets total. From strip sets, cut:
- 8—2½" × 4½" units
- 8—2½" × 6½" units

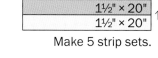

Make 5 strip sets.

2½" × 4½" Unit
Cut 8.

2½" × 6½" Unit
Cut 8.

(B) Sew together two light 1½" × 20" strips, a blue 5½" × 20" strip, and a blue 1½" × 20" strip to make a strip set. Press toward the blue strips. Cut 8—1½" × 8½"-wide Strip Units.

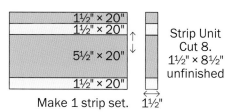

Make 1 strip set.  1½"

Strip Unit
Cut 8.
1½" × 8½"
unfinished

## 4 Unit One–Make 4

Refer to the illustration below to lay out Unit One using:
- 2—3½" × 4½" background rectangles
- 2—2½" × 3½" background rectangles
- 1—1½" × 1½" blue square
- 2—1½" × 8½" Strip Units (from step 3)
- 1—Four Patch block (from step 2b)
- 1—Nine Patch block (from step 1e)
- 1—Seven Patch block
- 2 —of Unit B

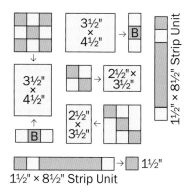

Join the pieces together as shown, then join rows together. Press. Repeat to make four total of Unit One that should measure 9½" × 9½" including seam allowances.

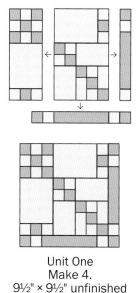

Unit One
Make 4.
9½" × 9½" unfinished

"Blue skies and snow-capped mountains, fluffy white clouds and sparkling blue water–Mother Nature is the best at creating breathtaking blue-and-white combinations." –Edyta

## 5 Unit Two–Make 8 (4 Left and 4 Right)

Refer to the illustration below to lay out one each of Unit Two (Left and Right) using:

- 1—3½" × 3½" background square
- 1—1½" × 7½" background rectangle
- 1—2½" × 3½" background rectangle
- 1—2½" × 2½" background square
- 1—3½" × 4½" background rectangle
- 1—Four Patch (from step 2b)
- 1 of Unit B (from step 1b)
- 2—Seven Patch (from step 1g)

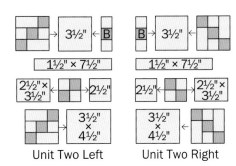

Unit Two Left        Unit Two Right

Join the pieces together as shown, then join rows together (do NOT sew Unit Two Left and Right segments to one another). Press. Repeat to make four total of Unit Two Left and four total of Unit Two Right that should measure 7½" × 9½" including seam allowances.

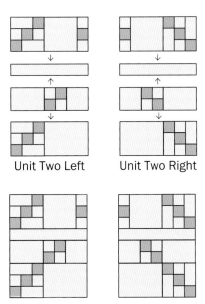

Unit Two Left        Unit Two Right

Unit Two Left and Right
Make 8 (4 Left and 4 Right).
7½" × 9½" unfinished

## 6 Unit Three–Make 4

Refer to the illustration below to lay out Unit Three using:

- 2—3½" × 4½" background rectangles
- 2—2½" × 2½" background squares
- 2—Four Patch blocks (from step 2b)
- 1—Nine Patch block (from step 1e)

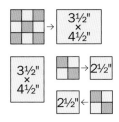

Join the pieces together as shown, then join rows together. Press. Repeat to make four total of Unit Three that should measure 7½" × 7½" including seam allowances.

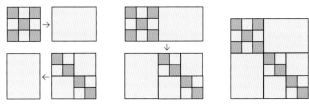

Unit Three
Make 4.
7½" × 7½" unfinished

## 7 Unit Four - Make 8 (4 Left and 4 Right)

Refer to the illustration below to lay out one each of Unit Four (Left and Right) using:

- 1—2½" × 3½" background rectangle
- 1—2½" × 5½" background rectangle
- 1—Seven Patch (from step 1g)

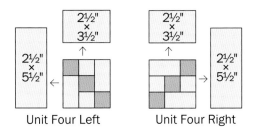

Unit Four Left        Unit Four Right

Join the pieces together as shown, then join rows together (do NOT sew Unit Four Left and Right segments to one another). Press. Repeat to make four total of Unit Four Left and four total of Unit Four Right that should measure 5½" × 5½" including seam allowances.

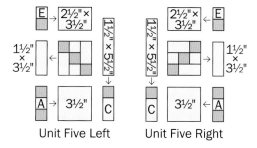

Unit Four Left    Unit Four Right

Unit Four Left and Right
Make 8 (4 Left and 4 Right).
5½" × 5½" unfinished

**8**  **Unit Five–Make 8 (4 Left and 4 Right)**
Refer to the illustration below to lay out one each of Unit Five (Left and Right) using:
- 1—3½" × 3½" background square
- 1—1½" × 5½" background rectangle
- 1—1½" × 3½" background rectangle
- 1—2½" × 3½" background rectangle
- 1 of Unit A (from step 1a)
- 1 of Unit C (from step 1c)
- 1 of Unit E (from step 2a)
- 1—Seven Patch (from step 1g)

Unit Five Left    Unit Five Right

Join the pieces together as shown, then join rows together (do NOT sew Unit Five Left and Right segments to one another). Press. Repeat to make four total of Unit Five Left and four total of Unit Five Right that should measure 5½" × 8½" including seam allowances.

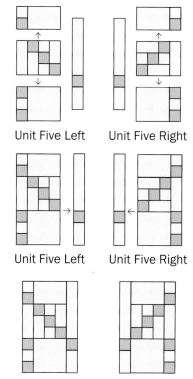

Unit Five Left    Unit Five Right

Unit Five Left    Unit Five Right

Unit Five Left and Right
Make 8 (4 Left and 4 Right).
5½" × 8½" unfinished

Pay attention to the pressing arrows on the illustrations as you are piecing the units. Pressing seams in the correct direction will make joining the units together easier.

## 9 Unit Six–Make 4

Refer to the illustration below to lay out Unit Six using:

- 2—2½" × 2½" background squares
- 2—2½" × 6½" background rectangles
- 1—Four Patch blocks (from step 2b)
- 1—Seven Patch blocks (from step 1g)
- 2 of Unit E (from step 2a)
- 1—3½" × 6½" Strip Unit (from step 1h)
- 1—3½" × 2½" Strip Unit (from step 1h)
- 1—3½" × 4½" Strip Unit (from step 1h)

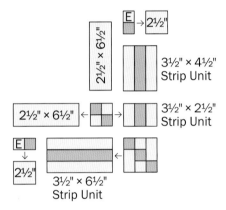

Join the pieces together as shown, then join rows together. (Leave Unit Six in two sections with the final seam unsewn.) Press. Repeat to make four total of Unit Six.

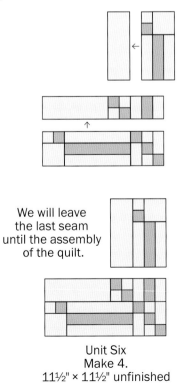

We will leave the last seam until the assembly of the quilt.

Unit Six
Make 4.
11½" × 11½" unfinished

## 10 Unit Seven–Make 8 (4 Left and 4 Right)

Refer to the illustration below to lay out one each of Unit Seven (Left and Right) using:

- 1—4½" × 4½" background square
- 1—4½" × 17½" background rectangle
- 1—2½" × 3½" background rectangle
- 1—2½" × 8½" background rectangle
- 1—1½" × 2½" background rectangle
- 1—1½" × 4½" blue rectangle
- 1—2½" × 6½" Strip Unit (from step 3a)
- 2—Four Patch blocks (from step 2b)

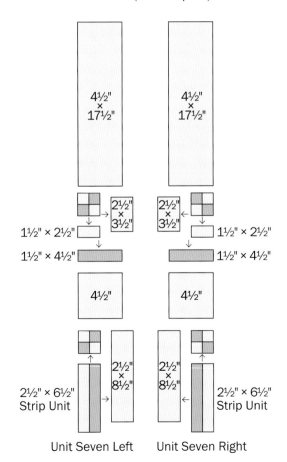

Unit Seven Left          Unit Seven Right

Join the pieces together as shown, then join rows together (do NOT sew Unit Seven Left and Right segments to one another). Press. Repeat to make four total of Unit Seven Left and four total of Unit Seven Right that should measure 4½" × 33½" including seam allowances.

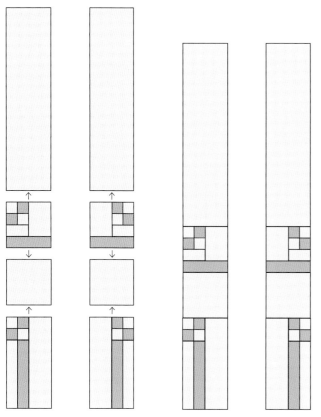

Unit Seven Left and Right
Make 8 (4 Left and 4 Right).
4½" × 33½" unfinished

## 11 Unit Seven Center–Make 4

Refer to the illustration below to lay out Unit Seven Center using:

- 2—1½" × 3½" background rectangles
- 1—Nine Patch block (from step 1e)
- 1—1½" × 1½" blue square

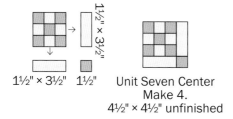

Unit Seven Center
Make 4.
4½" × 4½" unfinished

Join the pieces together as shown, then join rows together. Press. Repeat to make four total of Unit Seven Center that should measure 4½" × 4½" including seam allowances.

## 12 Unit Eight–Make 8 (4 Left and 4 Right)

Refer to the illustration below to lay out one each of Unit Eight (Left and Right) using:

- 1—2½" × 10½" light rectangle
- 2—2½" × 3½" light rectangles
- 3—1½" × 2½" light rectangles
- 1—1½" × 3½" light rectangle
- 4—Four Patch blocks (from step 2b)
- 1—Eight Patch blocks (from step 1g)
- 1—Unit D (from step 1d)
- 1—2½" × 2½" light square
- 1—Unit E (from step 2a)

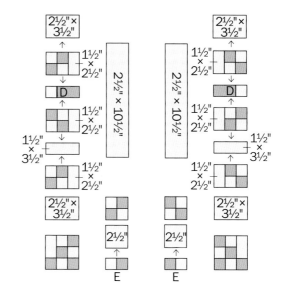

Join the pieces together as shown below, then join rows together (do NOT sew Unit Eight Left and Right segments to one another). Press. Repeat to make four total of Unit Eight Left and four total of Unit Eight Right that should measure 5½" × 15½" including seam allowances.

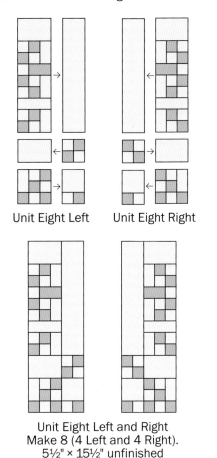

Unit Eight Left     Unit Eight Right

Unit Eight Left and Right
Make 8 (4 Left and 4 Right).
5½" × 15½" unfinished

13 **Unit Nine–Make 8 (4 Left and 4 Right)**
Refer to the illustration below to lay out one each of Unit Nine (Left and Right) using:

- 1—3½" × 6½" background rectangle
- 1—2½" × 6½" background rectangle
- 1—2½" × 3½" background rectangle
- 2—1½" × 3½" background rectangles
- 2—Four Patch blocks (from step 2b)
- 3—Seven Patch blocks (from step 1g)
- 1—2½" × 4½" Strip Unit (from step 3a)

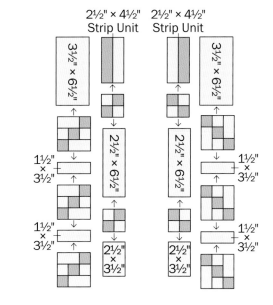

## 14 Unit Ten–Make 4

Refer to the illustration to lay out Unit Ten using:

- 2—5½" × 5½" background squares
- 2—2½" × 3½" background rectangles
- 1—Four Patch block (from step 2b)
- 1—Seven Patch block(from step 1g)

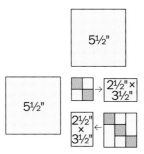

Join the pieces together as shown, then join rows together (do NOT sew Unit Nine Left and Right segments to one another). Press. Repeat to make four total of Unit Nine Left and four total of Unit Nine Right that should measure 5½" × 17½" including seam allowances.

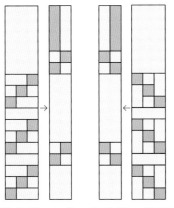

Unit Nine Left     Unit Nine Right

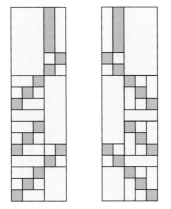

Unit Nine Left     Unit Nine Right

Unit Nine Left and Right
Make 8 (4 Left and 4 Right).
5½" × 17½" unfinished

Join the pieces together as shown, then join rows together. (Leave Unit Ten in two sections with the final seam unsewn.) Press. Repeat to make four total of Unit Ten.

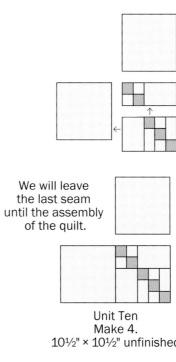

We will leave the last seam until the assembly of the quilt.

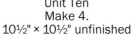

Unit Ten
Make 4.
10½" × 10½" unfinished

Label each unit with its corresponding number and left or right designation as you complete them. You'll be happy you've done so when it's time to assemble the quilt top.

15 **Unit Eleven–Make 8 (4 Left and 4 Right)**
Refer to the illustration below to lay out one each of Unit Eleven (Left and Right) using:

- 1—2½" × 12½" background rectangle
- 1 of Unit E (from step 2a)
- 1—1½" × 2½" blue rectangle
- 2—1½" × 2½" light rectangles
- 1—Four Patch block (from Step 2b; note that this block is only added to Unit Eleven Left)

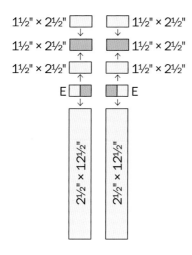

Join the pieces together as shown, then join rows together. (Leave Unit Eleven Left in two sections with the final seam unsewn.) Press. Repeat to make four total of Unit Eleven Left and four total of Unit Eleven Right .

We will leave the last seam until the assembly of the quilt.

Unit Eleven Left and Right
Make 8 (4 Left and 4 Right).
2½" × 16½" unfinished

16 **Unit Twelve–Make 8 (4 Left and 4 Right)**
Refer to the illustration below to lay out one each of Unit Twelve (Left and Right) using:

- 1—9½" × 17½" background rectangle (Left only)
- 1—9½" × 26½" background rectangle (Right only)
- 1—3½" × 7½" background rectangle
- 1—4½" × 9½" background rectangle
- 1 of Unit A (from step 1a)
- 1 of Unit B (from step 1b)

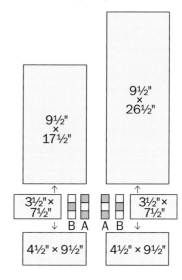

Join the pieces together as shown below, then join rows together. Press. Repeat to make four total of Unit Twelve (Left) and four total of Unit Twelve (Right).

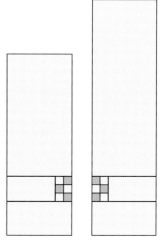

Unit Twelve Left and Right
Make 8 (4 Left and 4 Right).
Left – 9½" × 24½" unfinished
Right – 9½" × 33½" unfinished

 "Quilters are like snowflakes—no two are exactly the same. And I love that. There is always something new that we can learn from one another." –Edyta

**17** **Assemble the quadrants of the quilt:** When positioning units, pay close attention to the shading of dark to light from the center of the quilt outward if you wish to mimic the original quilt.

(A) Referring to the diagram below, sew together a 1½" × 4½" blue rectangle, a 1½" × 12½" blue rectangle, and two 1½" background squares to make a small sashing strip. Repeat to make a total of eight small sashing strips. (You will use two per quadrant of the quilt.)

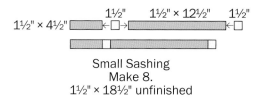

Small Sashing
Make 8.
1½" × 18½" unfinished

(B) Referring to the diagram below, arrange the following to create one quadrant of the quilt top:
- 1—1½" × 1½" blue square
- 1 Each of Unit 1, Unit 2 (Left & Right), Unit 3, Unit 4 (Left & Right), Unit 5 (Left & Right), Unit 6 (in two pieces), Unit 7 (Left & Right), Unit 7 Center, Unit 8 (Left & Right), Unit 9 (Left & Right), Unit 10, Unit 11 (Left & Right), and Unit 12 (Left & Right).
- 2—Small sashing Strips (from Step 17a)

(C) Following the diagram below, sew the rows together. Begin by sewing units into groups. Sew units 1, 2, and 3 together to make Group A. Next, sew units 4 (left), 5, and 6 together; then repeat with units 4 (right), 5 and 6 to complete Group B.

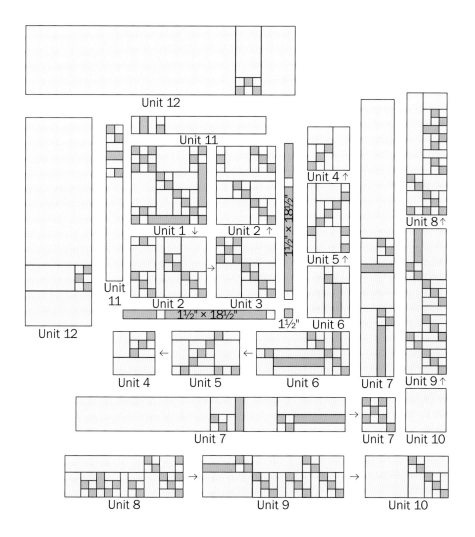

As you begin to assemble a quadrant of the quilt, press several times along the way to ensure smooth, flat edges before joining more pieces in the section.

Lastly, sew together units 8 (left), 9, and 10 together; then sew units 8 (right), 9, and 10 to complete Group C. Follow arrows for pressing or press your seams open.

(D) Add units 11 (left & right) to Group A.

(E) Add the small sashing strips and Group B to Group A as shown below.

(F) Join units 12 (left & right), 7 (left, center & right) to the Group A/B unit as shown. Complete the quadrant by adding Group C (left and right) to the right side and bottom edge of the unit to complete one quadrant of the quilt top. The pieced quadrant should measure 42½" × 42½" including the seam allowances.

(G) Repeat steps 17(b)–(f) to make a total of four quadrants.

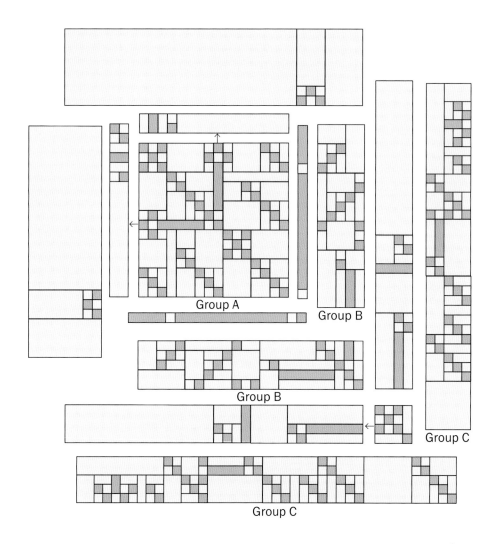

Group A

Group B

Group B

Group C

Group C

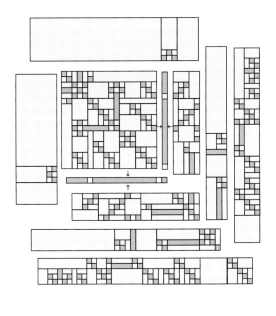

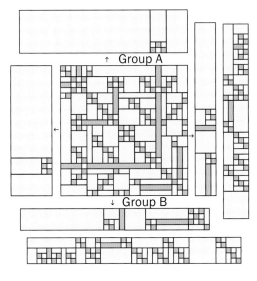

↑ Group A

↓ Group B

Unit 12 Right

Unit 12 Left

Unit 7

Group C

↓ Unit 7

Unit 7 ↑

Group C

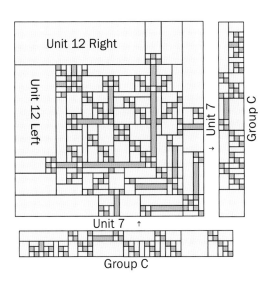

"Snuggled under this giant snowflake quilt, you can't help but have sweet dreams." –Edyta

18 **Assemble the sashing:** Referring to the diagram below, sew together a 1½" × 36½" blue sashing strip, a 1½" × 3½" blue rectangle, a 1½" × 3½" background rectangle, and a 1½" × 1½" background square to make a long sashing strip. Repeat to make a total of four long sashing strips.

19 **Assemble the quilt top:** Referring to the diagram, arrange the four quadrants of the quilt, the four long sashing strips, and a 1½" × 1½" blue square. Join the pieces in rows, then sew together the rows to make the quilt top. The quilt top should measure 85½" × 85½" including the seam allowances.

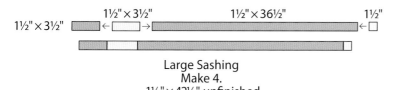

Large Sashing
Make 4.
1½" × 42½" unfinished

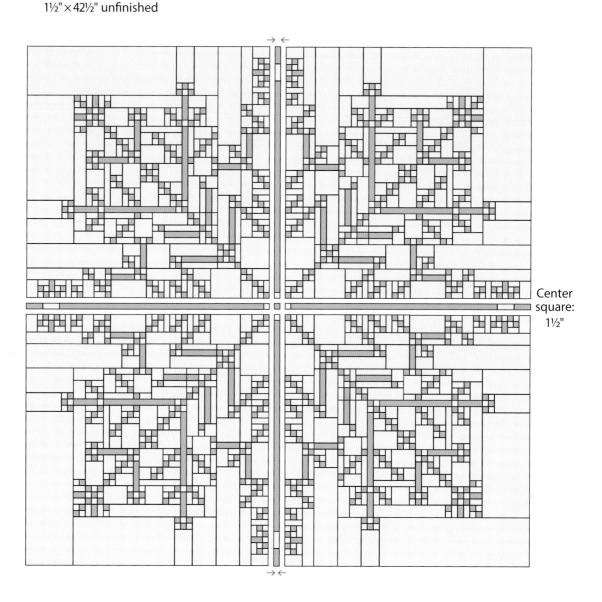

Center
square:
1½"

 "I'm proud to carry on my family tradition that fabric and threads have seamlessly stitched together through the generations. And most of all, I wish the same for you and yours." –Edyta

**20** **Add the borders:** Sew the 2" × 85½" borders to opposite sides of the quilt center. Then join the 2" × 88½" borders to the top and bottom.

**21** **Quilting:** Layer quilt according to the instructions on page 143. Quilt as desired.

**22** **Binding:** Use the 2½"-wide blue strips to bind the quilt following the instructions on page 143.

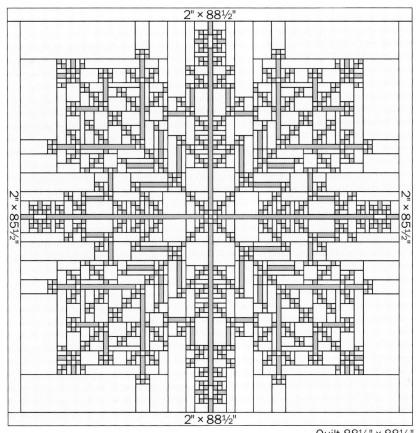

2" × 88½"

2" × 85½"

2" × 85½"

2" × 88½"

Quilt 88½" × 88½"

# bars and stripes

Finish this quilt quick as a wink, before Jack Frost is nipping at your nose. It's a wonderful way to use up treasured scraps of blue and cream prints.

**Quilt is 60½" × 81½"**

## fabric requirements

**Strips:**
2 yards total of assorted blue fabric
4½ yards total of assorted of light fabric
**Binding:** ⅔ yard of blue fabric
**Backing:** 5 yards
**Batting:** 67" × 88"

*Note: WOF designates the width of fabric from selvedge to selvedge (approximately 42" wide).*

## fabric cutting

**Blue Fabric:**
From assorted fabrics, cut:
• 40—1½" × WOF strips

**Light Fabric:**
From assorted fabrics, cut:
• 20—1½" × WOF strips
• 24—3½" × WOF strips

**Binding:**
• 8—2½" × WOF blue strips

## construction

*Use a ¼" seam allowance. Press toward the blue strips or press seams open.*

1 Sew together six assorted blue 1½" × WOF strips end to end to make a long blue strip. Cut the long strip into four 1½" × 60½" scrappy blue rows. Repeat to make a total of 26 scrappy blue rows. (You can begin your second long strip with any remaining piece of the first long strip you made. This will stagger the joins differently as you progress on your scrappy blue rows.)

2 In the same manner, sew together six assorted light 1½" × WOF strips end to end to make a long 1½"-wide light strip. Cut the long strip into four 1½" × 60½" scrappy light rows. Repeat to make a total of 13 scrappy 1½"-wide light rows.

3 In the same manner, sew together six assorted light 3½" × WOF strips end to end to make a long 3½"-wide light strip. Cut the long strip into four 3½" × 60½" scrappy light rows. Repeat to make a total of 14 scrappy 3½"-wide light rows.

4 (A) To join the rows, start by sewing together two blue 1½" × 60½" scrappy rows and one 1½" × 60½" light scrappy row. To keep your rows straight, consider reversing the stitching direction each time. Press seam allowances toward the blue strips. The three-row set should measure 3½" × 60½" including seam allowances. Repeat to make a total of 13 three-rows sets.

(B) Alternating between the three-row sets made above and 3½" × 60½" scrappy light rows, join the rows together, beginning and ending with a 3½" × 60½" scrappy light row to complete the quilt top. Again, to help keep your rows straight as you sew, reverse directions as you add each row.

5 **Quilting:** Layer quilt according to the instructions on page 143. Quilt as desired.

6 **Binding:** Use the 2½"-wide blue strips to bind the quilt following the instructions on page 143.

# maze

A center medallion at the heart of the quilt is a perfect spot to showcase a large-scale print. Repeating that print in borders as you add rounds of pieced patchwork captures even more attention on an heirloom your family will treasure.

**Quilt is 88½" × 88½". Finished center block is 12" × 12".**

# fabric requirements

Please read through all directions before starting. Letters in (parentheses) refer to the position of fabrics in the finished quilt. Letter designations are repeated in cutting and instruction diagrams to aid in assembly.

**Center (A) and Borders (N, O, X):**
   3 yards of large-scale light print (Note: border strips are cut lengthwise)

**Scrappy Blocks (C, D, E, F, K, P, Q, R, S):**
   12—fat quarters (18" × 21") of assorted blues and teals
   8—fat quarters (18" × 21") of assorted lights

**Setting Triangles (B, L, M, V) and Binding:** 1¾ yards of dark blue print

**Triangles (G):** ⅓ yard of teal large print

**Background (H, I) :** 1 yard of light print 1

**Squares (J):** ⅓ yard of blue print

**Border (T, W):** 1¼ yards of teal blue print

**Triangles (U):** ½ yard of light print 2

**Backing:** 8 yards

**Batting:** 95" × 95"

WOF designates the width of fabric from selvedge to selvedge (approximately 42" wide).

# fabric cutting

**Large-Scale Light Print:**

A:  1—12½" square for center block

N:  2—4½" × 40½" strips cut lengthwise for Border Two

O:  2—4½" × 48½" strips cut lengthwise for Border Two

X:  4—4½" × 80½" strips cut lengthwise for Border Seven

**From assorted blue and teal fat quarters, cut:**

D:  4—2⅞" squares, cut once diagonally to make eight half-square triangles for center block

E:  8—2½" squares for center block and Border Six cornerstones

F:  4—2½" squares for Border Four cornerstones

K:  136—3⅜" squares for Border Five

P:  24—4⅞" squares, cut once diagonally to make 48 half-square triangles for Border Three

R:  4—4½" squares for Border Three cornerstones

S:  4—4½" squares for Border Seven cornerstones

**From assorted light fat quarters, cut:**

C:  8—2⅞" squares, cut once diagonally to make 16 half-square triangles for center block

K:  68— 3⅜" squares for Border Five

Q:  24—4⅞" squares, cut once diagonally to make 48 half-square triangles for Border Three

**Dark Blue Print:**

B:  12—2⅞" squares, cut once diagonally to make 24 half-square triangles for center block

L:  16—5¼" squares, cut in half twice diagonally to make 64 quarter-square triangles for Border One

M:  8—2⅞" squares, cut once diagonally to make 16 half-square triangles for Border One

V:  19—5¼" squares, cut in half twice diagonally to make 76 quarter-square triangles for Border Five

10—2½" × WOF strips for binding

**Teal Large Print:**

G:  4—8⅞" squares, cut once diagonally to make eight half-square triangles for center Flying Geese star points

**Light Print 1:**

H:  1—17¼" square, cut in half twice diagonally to make four quarter-square triangles for center Flying Geese

I:  4— 8½" squares for center block background

**Blue Print:**

J:  36—3⅜" squares for Border One

**Teal Blue Print:**

T:  6—2½" × WOF strips for Border Four

W:  8—2½" × WOF strips for Border Six

**Light Print 2:**

U:  15— 5¼" squares, cut in half twice diagonally to make 60 quarter-square triangles for Border Five

# construction

*Use a ¼" seam allowance. Press in the direction of the arrows.*

**1** **Center Block:** To make one of Unit 1, you will need six blue B triangles, four light C triangles, and two blue D triangles. Referring to the diagrams below and noting the directional changes, sew together the triangles in pairs to make triangle squares; press all seam allowances toward the darks. Then sew the triangle squares together in a row to complete Unit 1. Repeat to make four of Unit 1.

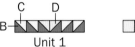

Unit 1

**2** Sew a Unit 1 to the top and bottom of the 12½" large-scale print center square. Add an E cornerstone to each end of the remaining Unit 1 pieces, then sew those Unit 1 pieces to the left and right sides of the center block as shown. Press seam allowances toward the center.

**3** To make one Unit 2, sew a blue G triangle to opposite sides of a light H triangle as shown at right. Press toward blue. Repeat to make four of Unit 2.

Sew a Unit 2 to the top and bottom of the center square. Add a light I cornerstone to each end of the remaining Unit 2 pieces, then sew those Unit 2 pieces to the left and right sides of the center block as shown. Press the seam allowances toward the outside of the block.

Unit 2

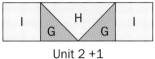

Unit 2 +1

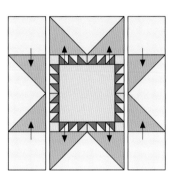

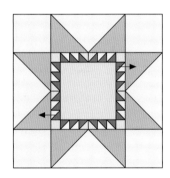

**4** **Border One:** To make Border One, you will need 64 dark blue L triangles, 36 blue J squares, and 16 dark blue M triangles. Follow the diagrams below to assemble two short borders of eight J squares and two long borders of 10 J squares. First, sew the J and L pieces together in diagonal strips, adding the M corner pieces last. Press away from the J squares in each strip, and in one direction for each border.

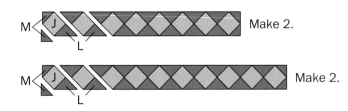

Make 2.

Make 2.

**5** Sew the short Border One strips to the top and bottom of the quilt center; press seam allowances toward quilt center. In the same manner, sew the long Border One strips to the remaining sides of the quilt and press toward quilt center.

**6** Border Two: Sew the 4½" × 40½" large-scale light N strips to the top and bottom of the quilt center; press toward the outside of the quilt. Then sew the 4½" × 48½" large-scale light O strips to the remaining edges and press in the same manner.

**7** Border Three: To make one Unit 3, you will need 12 light Q triangles and 12 blue P triangles. Referring to the diagram below and noting the directional change, sew together the triangles in pairs to make triangle squares; press all seam allowances toward the blues. Then sew triangle squares together in a row to complete Unit 3. Repeat to make four of Unit 3.

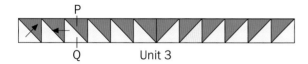

Unit 3

**8** Sew a Unit 3 to the top and bottom of the quilt center. Add a blue R cornerstones to each end of the remaining Unit 3 pieces, then sew them to the remaining edges of the quilt center as shown. Press seam allowances toward the quilt center.

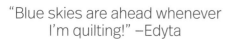

"Blue skies are ahead whenever I'm quilting!" —Edyta

Unit 3

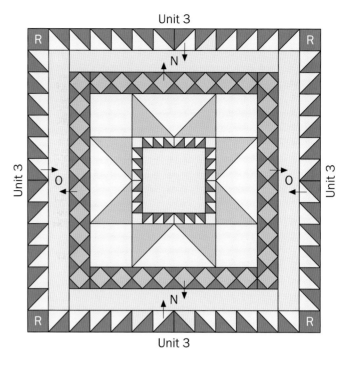

**9** Border Four: Piece together three of the 2½" × WOF teal blue print T strips end to end to make a long strip. Subcut that strip into two 2½" × 56½" border strips. Repeat with the remaining T strips to make a total of four 2½" × 56½" border strips. Sew a border strip to the top and bottom of the quilt center. Add blue F cornerstones to each end of the remaining two border strips, then sew them to the left and right side of the quilt center. Press the seam allowances toward the outside of the quilt.

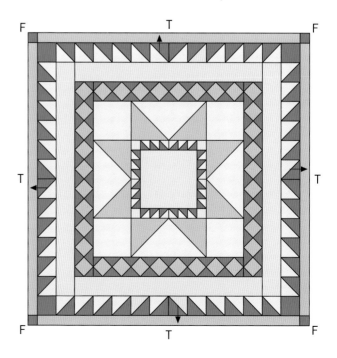

111

10 **Border Five:** To make one Border Five strip, you will need 34 assorted blue and teal K squares, 17 assorted light K squares, 19 dark blue V triangles, and 15 light U triangles. Referring to the diagram below for positions, sew together two blue K squares and one light K square into a set of three. Noting the orientation of the pieces, add a blue V triangle and a light U triangle to opposite ends of the set to make a Unit 4. Repeat to make a total of 15 of Unit 4. Press seam allowances in one direction, alternating directions with each strip. Use the remaining pieces to sew together Unit 5 as shown below. Then sew together 15 of Unit 4 and one

of Unit 5, making sure to keep the blue V triangles on the same edge, to make a Border Five strip. Repeat to make a total of four Border Five strips.

11 Sew a Border Five strip to each side of the quilt, pinning first to match the center of each strip with the quilt center. Sew the top and the bottom borders on first, leaving a ¼" seam allowance unsewn at each end. Repeat to add the remaining two Border Five strips to opposite edges in the same manner. Miter the corners to complete and press seam allowances toward Border Four.

**12** **Border Six:** Piece together two 2½" × WOF teal blue print W strips end to end to make a long strip. Subcut that strip into a 2½" × 76½" border strip. Repeat with the remaining W strips to make a total of four 2½" × 76½" border strips. Sew a border strip to the top and bottom of the quilt center. Add blue E cornerstones to each end of the remaining two border strips, then sew them to the left and right side of the quilt center. Press the seam allowances toward the outside of the quilt.

**13** **Border Seven:** Sew large-scale print 4½" × 80½" X strips to the top and bottom of the quilt center. Add a blue S cornerstone to each end of the remaining two X strips, then sew these borders to the remaining edges of the quilt center. Press seam allowances toward the quilt center.

**14** **Quilting:** Layer quilt according to the instructions on page 143. Quilt as desired.

**15** **Binding:** Use the 2½"-wide blue strips to bind the quilt following the instructions on page 143.

# norway

After a day of alpine adventures, curl up beside
a crackling fireplace and snuggle up beneath a two-color beauty
that's both restful and relaxing.

**Quilt is 60½" × 60½"**

## fabric requirements

**Blocks and Binding:** 1½ yards of light fabric
**Blocks and Background:** 3 yards of blue fabric
**Backing:** 3¾ yards
**Batting:** 67" × 67"

## fabric cutting

**Note:** Read assembly directions before cutting pieces. Borders are cut to exact length required plus ¼" seam allowances. WOF designates the width of fabric from selvedge to selvedge (approximately 42" wide).

**Light Fabric**
- 11—2½" × WOF strips
  From those strips, cut:
  - 162—2½" × 2½" A squares

**Blue Fabric**
- 5—10½" × WOF strips
  From those strips, cut:
  - 18—10½" B squares
- 12—2½" × WOF strips
  From those strips, cut:
  - 72—2½" × 6½" B strips
- 5—2½" × WOF strips
  From those strips, cut:
  - 72—2½" × 2½" B squares

**Binding**
- 7—2½" × WOF strips

**Backing**
- 2—68" × WOF strips
  (Sew together and trim to make a 68" × 68" backing.)

*"Find beauty in the ordinary every day. Sometimes the simplest quilts are the ones I love the most."*
—Edyta

## construction

*Use a ¼" seam allowance. Press in the direction of the arrows.*

1 **Block Assembly:** Sew a 2½" light A square to each side of a 2½" blue B square to make the top row. Repeat to make the bottom row. Sew a 2½" blue B square to each side of a 2½" light A square to make the middle row. Sew the three rows together to make Unit 1. Unit 1 should measure 6½" square including seam allowances. Repeat to make 18 total of Unit 1.

Unit 1
Make 18.

2 Sew a 2½" light A square to each end of a 2½" × 6½" blue B strip to make the top row. Repeat to make the bottom row. Sew a 2½" × 6½" blue B strip to each side of a Unit 1 to make the middle row. Sew the three rows together to complete Block One. Block One should measure 10½" square including seam allowances. Repeat to make 18 total of Block One.

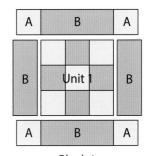

Block 1
Make 18.

3 **Quilt-Top Assembly:** Sew together three of Block One and three 10½" blue B squares, alternating them as shown, to make Row One. Repeat to make Row Three and Row Five.

4 Sew together three 10½" blue B squares and three of Block One, alternating them, to make Row Two. Repeat to make Row Four and Row Six.

5 Join the six rows together in numerical order to complete the quilt top.

6 **Quilting:** Layer quilt according to the instructions on page 143. Quilt as desired.

7 **Binding:** Use the 2½"-wide blue strips to bind the quilt following the instructions on page 143.

| B | Block 1 | B | Block 1 | B | Block 1 |
| Block 1 | B | Block 1 | B | Block 1 | B |
| B | Block 1 | B | Block 1 | B | Block 1 |
| Block 1 | B | Block 1 | B | Block 1 | B |
| B | Block 1 | B | Block 1 | B | Block 1 |
| Block 1 | B | Block 1 | B | Block 1 | B |

# sky and sea

A simplified construction method lets you create a look you'll love with a single block. The luxe look is created with the spin of the blocks as you place them!

**Quilt is 40½" × 48½"**

# fabric requirements

**Blocks:**
   5—fat quarters (18" × 21") of assorted blues
   1½ yards of light print
**Binding:** ½ yard of blue print
**Backing:** 3 yards
**Batting:** 47" × 55"

# fabric cutting

**Note:** Read assembly directions before cutting. WOF designates the width of fabric from selvedge to selvedge (approximately 42" wide).

### Assorted Blues

From *each* fat quarter referring to the diagram at right, cut:
- 6—4½" × 4½" squares
- 4—2⅞" × 18" strips
  From those strips, subcut 24—2⅞" squares; cut once diagonally to make 48 half-square triangles

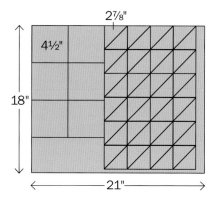

Cutting Chart for Blue Fat Quarter

### Light Print

Referring to the diagram at right, cut:
- 4—4½" × WOF strips
  From those strips, subcut 30—4½" squares
- 9—2⅞" × WOF strips
  From those strips, subcut 120—2⅞" squares; cut once diagonally to make 240 half-square triangles

### Binding:
- 5—2½" × WOF blue strips

"I love to play around with colors and fabrics. Even when I am making a two-color quilt, I enjoy pulling a variety of light, medium, and dark prints in a mix of small to large designs to see which ones will give me the look I'm after." –Edyta

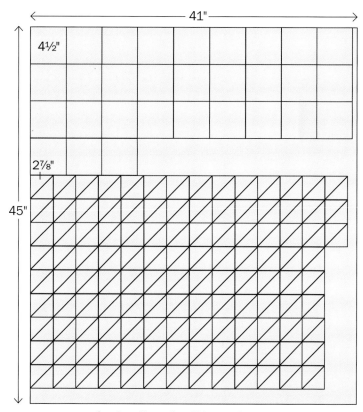

Cutting Chart for 1¼ yard light piece

# construction

*Use ¼" seam allowances. Press in the direction of the arrows.*

**1** Begin by making 2½" unfinished (2" finished) half-square triangles from assorted blues and the light print. Layer one blue and one light triangle right sides together. Sew using a ¼" seam allowance. Press your triangles open and trim the dog-ears. Repeat to make 240 half-square triangles total (48 from each blue fat quarter).

2⅞"

trim

trim

2½" × 2½" unfinished

**2** For one block, you will need: eight matching 2½" half-square triangles, one matching 4½" blue square, and one 4½" light square. Referring to the diagram, arrange and sew together the pieces to make one block. The finished block should be 8½" × 8½" including seam allowances. Repeat to make a total of 30 blocks.

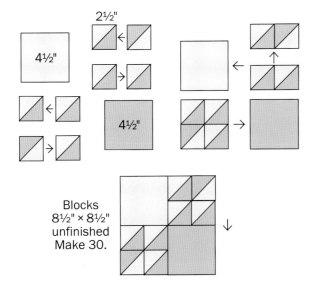

2½"

4½"

4½"

Blocks
8½" × 8½"
unfinished
Make 30.

**3** Referring to the diagram above right for placement and paying attention to the rotation of each block, arrange the blocks in six rows of five blocks each. Join the blocks into rows, pressing rows in opposite directions as indicated by arrows so that the seams will lock together when you join the rows. Then sew the rows together.

**4** **Quilting:** Layer quilt according to the instructions on page 143. Quilt as desired.

**5** **Binding:** Use the 2½"-wide blue strips to bind the quilt following the instructions on page 143.

# stardust

A frosty night has never felt warmer when you're tucked in under a magical sprinkling of quilted stardust. Your heart will be a flurry of good feelings.

**Quilt is 71" × 80"**

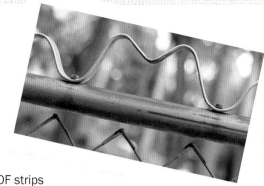

# fabric requirements

**Blues for Snowflakes:**
16—fat eighths (9" × 21")
**Light Background:** 6½ yards
**Border:** 1½ yards blue print
**Binding:** ⅔ yard dark blue
**Backing:** 4⅞ yards
**Batting:** 77" × 86"

# fabric cutting

**Note:** Read assembly directions before cutting. WOF designates the width of fabric from selvedge to selvedge (approximately 42" wide). Templates are on page 125.

## Snowflakes

From the blue fat eighths, cut:
- 18—2½" × 21" strips (cut at least one strip from each fat eighth if you wish to have snowflakes made from matching blue fabrics)
- 69—1" × 21" strips
  Subcut the strips in half to make
  - 138—1" × 10½" strips (keep some matching sets of six together for matching snowflakes)

## Light Background

- 2—7½" × WOF strips
  From those strips, subcut
  - 4—7½" × 12½" rectangles
- 7—6¾" × WOF strips
  From those strips and using template A, cut 56 A triangles

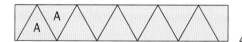

- 16—6¼" × WOF strips
  From those strips and using template B, cut 138 B triangles

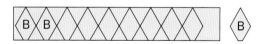

- 12—2¾" × WOF strips
  From those strips and using template C, cut 276 C triangles C

- 9—1½" × WOF strips
  Subcut those strips in half to make
  - 18—1½" × 21" strips

## Border

- 8—6" × WOF strips
  Sew two strips end-to-end to make a long strip. Make 4 long strips.

## Binding

- 8—2½" × WOF strips

*Use a ¼" seam allowance. Press in the direction of the arrows.*

# construction

1 **Snowflakes** (**Note:** Make some snowflakes with matching blues)

(A) Join a 2½" × 21" blue strip and a 1½" × 21" background strip as shown to make a strip set. Repeat to make 18 strips sets total.

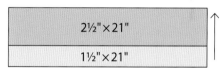

Make 18 strip sets.

(B) Use a 60° ruler or a template to cut a 60° angle at the beginning of one strip set as shown below. Repeat to cut the same angle on a total of 9 of the 18 strip sets made in step (A).

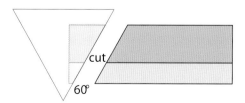

(**Note:** You may wish to keep matching sets of six together for steps C, E, and I to create matching blue fabric snowflakes.)

121

(C) Align the 1" line of a ruler with the just-cut angle as shown. Cut 16 1"-wide D units from the strip set. Repeat with the eight additional strip sets previously cut in step (B) to make 138 D units total.

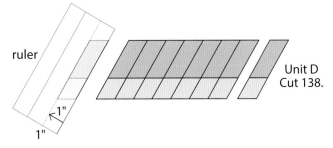

(D) Use a 60° ruler or a template to cut a 60° angle (in the opposite direction as before) at the beginning of one of the remaining strip sets as shown below. Repeat to cut the same angle on the remaining 8 strip sets made in step (A).

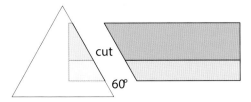

(E) Align the 1" line of a ruler with the just-cut angle as shown. Cut 16 1"-wide E units from the strip set. Repeat with the eight additional strip sets previously cut in step (D) to make 138 E units total.

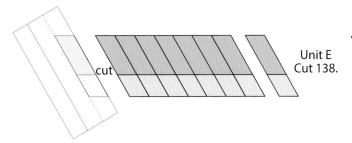

(F) Sew Unit D to the left side of a C background triangle as shown. Trim. Repeat to make a total of 138 C/D Units.

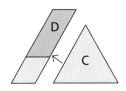  

Make 138.

(G) In the same manner, sew Unit E to the right side of a C background triangle as shown. Trim. Repeat to make a total of 138 C/E Units.

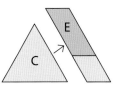  

Make 138.

(H) Add a C/E Unit and a C/D Unit to opposite sides of a B background piece as shown, matching prints as desired. Repeat to make 138 total.

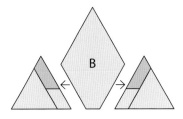 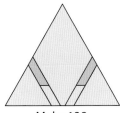

Make 138.

(I) Add a 1" × 10½" blue strip, matching prints as desired, to the step (H) unit to make a snowflake section. Press and trim as shown below. Repeat to make 138 Snowflake Sections total.

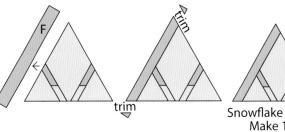 

Snowflake Section
Make 138.

(J) Join six Snowflake Sections as shown to make a Snowflake. Press seam allowances in direction of arrows. Repeat to make a total of 23 Snowflakes.

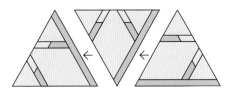
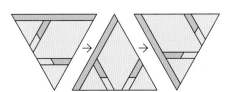

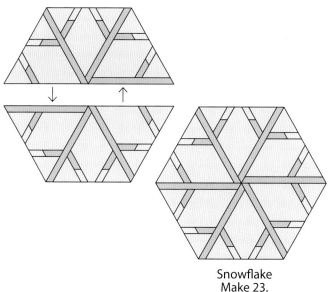

Snowflake
Make 23.

**Note:** After sewing halves together, gently open the center seam allowance from the back to allow the seams to press in the direction of the arrows.

(K) Join five Snowflakes and 12 background A triangles to make column A as shown. Trim the edges of the column ends leaving a ¼" seam allowance. Repeat to make three of Column A. Then join four snowflakes, 10 background A triangles, and two 12½" × 7½" background rectangles to make a column B as shown. Repeat to make two of Column B. Join the columns as shown Press seam allowances toward column B.

"These snowflakes won't melt away in the springtime. Once you capture them in fabric, they are everlasting."
–Edyta

2 **Borders:** Measure across the vertical center of the quilt for the best measurement. Trim two border strips to this length. Add to the sides of the quilt. Measure across the horizontal center for the best measurement. Trim two border strips to this length. Add to the top and bottom of the quilt. Press seam allowances toward the borders.

3 **Quilting:** Layer quilt according to the instructions on page 143. Quilt as desired.

4 **Binding:** Use the 2½"-wide blue strips to bind the quilt following the instructions on page 143.

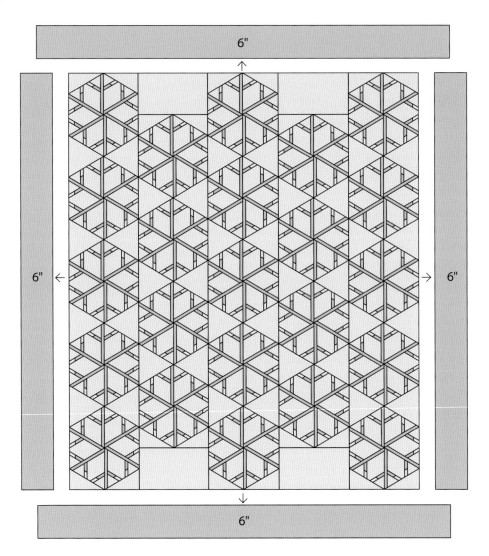

Measuring across the center of your quilt before cutting your borders will help eliminate any slight differences in length you may get if you were to measure opposite edges.

| TEMPLATE | DESCRIPTION | # TO CUT |
|----------|-------------|----------|
| A | Background | 56 |
| B | Background | 138 |
| C | Background | 276 |

**Stardust**
Template C

**Stardust**
Template A

Top

**Stardust**
Template B

# home for the holidays

If Winter Village is a family favorite quilt in your home
for the holidays, then consider making a mini pillow version
to send home with your family members.

**Pillow is 18" × 18"**

## fabric requirements

**Block and Binding:**
1 yard total of assorted blues
**Background, Backing, and Border:** 1¼ yards total
of assorted lights
**Batting:** 20" × 20"
**18" pillow form**
**Optional:** Silhouettes laser-cut appliqués
(LBQ-0638-S) and (LBQ-0393-S) rather than
cutting your own appliqués (Appliqué Templates
are on pages 82 and 83.)

## fabric cutting

### SMALL HOUSE
**From assorted blues:**
• 1—4½" × 4½" square for roof
• 1—2½" × 6½" rectangle
• 1—1½" × 6½" rectangle
• 1—1½" × 4½" rectangle
• 2—1½" × 1½" squares
**From assorted lights:**
• 1—2½" × 4½" rectangle
• 1—1½" × 2½" rectangle
• 2—1½" × 1½" squares

### LARGE HOUSE
**From assorted blues:**
• 1—4" × 7½" rectangle
• 4—1½" × 10" rectangles
• 9—1½" × 2½" rectangles
**From assorted lights:**
• 2—4" × 4" squares for roof
• 6—1½" × 3" rectangles for window

**Backing** (see diagram below for most efficient cutting):
• 1—21" × 21" square for the backing
• 2—18" × 12" rectangles for the pillow back

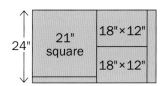

**Border:**
• 2—3" × 13½" light strips
• 1—3" × 18" light strip
• 1—2½" × 18" light strip
• 1—2" × 13½" light strip

**Binding:**
• 2—2½" × width of fabric blue strips

## construction

*Use a ¼" seam allowance. Press in the direction of the arrows or press seam allowances open.*

1 Arrange one blue 1½" square, one light 1½" square for window, one blue 1½" × 4½" rectangle, one blue 2½" × 6½" rectangle, one blue 1½" × 6½" rectangle, one blue 4½" square for roof, one light 1½" × 2½" rectangle, one blue 1½" square, one light 1½" square, and one light 2½" × 4½" rectangle as shown. Join the pieces in sections, then join the sections to make the Small House unit. Follow arrows as shown below for pressing. The unit should be 4½" × 13½" including seam allowances.

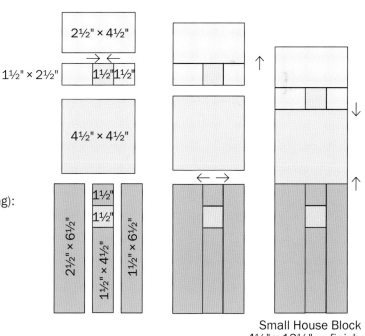

Small House Block
4½" × 13½" unfinished

2 To make the roof, you'll need two matching light 4" squares and one blue 4" × 7½" rectangle. Draw a diagonal line from corner to corner on the wrong side of a 4" square. Layer the marked square right sides together on the corner of the 4" × 7½" blue rectangle as shown. Sew on the marked line. Press the light print open to the corner to form a triangle. Repeat with the opposite 4" square on the opposite end of the blue rectangle to make the roof unit.

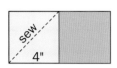 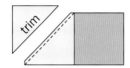

Rectangle
4" × 7½" unfinished
Make 1.

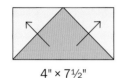

3 Arrange six light 1½" × 3" rectangles for windows, nine blue 1½" × 2" pieces, four blue 1½" × 10" rectangles, and one 4" × 7½" roof unit. Join the pieces in sections, then join the sections to make the Large House unit. Follow arrows as shown below for pressing. The unit should be 7½" × 13½" including seam allowances.

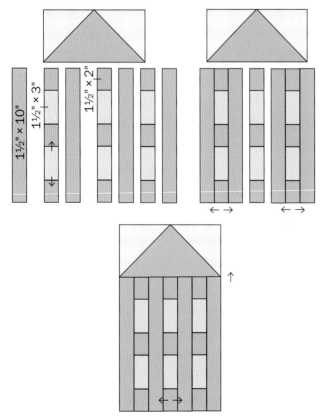

Large House Block
7½" × 13½" unfinished

4 Arrange two light 3" × 13½" border strips, a light 2" × 13½" border strips, the Small House unit, the Large House unit, and two light 3" × 18" border strips. Join the pieces in sections, then join the sections to make the pillow front. Press all seams toward the border strips. The pillow front should be 18" square including seam allowances.

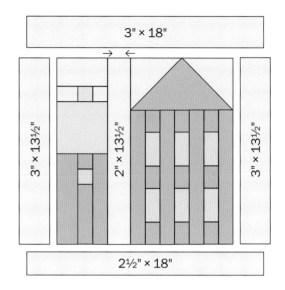

5 Appliqué: Select your favorite appliqué method to add the snowflakes, berries, branches, and bird from pages 82 and 83 to the pillow front block as shown.

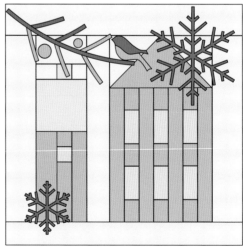

Pillow is 18" × 18"

6 Layer the pillow top on the batting and backing, wrong sides together. Quilt as desired. When finished quilting, trim the batting and backing even with the quilted pillow front.

7 **Pillow back:** Press one long side of a backing rectangle under 1", press. Then turn under 1" again; press. Topstitch. Repeat to make a second backing rectangle.

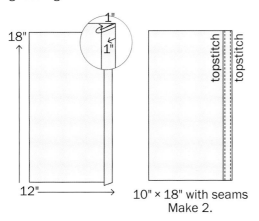

18"

1"
1"

12"

topstitch
topstitch

10" × 18" with seams
Make 2.

8 Place the quilted pillow top face down. Layer the two pillow backs, wrong sides together, atop the quilted pillow top and overlapping as shown. Baste around the outer edges to hold the Pillow backs and Pillow top together.

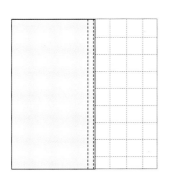

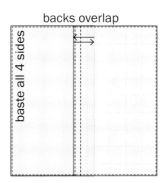

backs overlap

baste all 4 sides

9 **Binding:** Use the 2½"-wide blue strips to bind the pillow top as you would a quilt following the instructions on page 143. The center overlap of the pillow backs is left open for you to insert a pillow form through once the binding is complete.

Binding

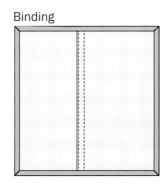

| TEMPLATE | DESCRIPTION | # TO CUT |
|---|---|---|
| A | Snowflake Small | 1 blue |
| B | Snowflake Large | 1 blue |
| D | Stem Medium | 1 blue |
| E | Stem Small | 6 blue |
| F | Circle Small | 1 blue |
| G | Circle Large | 1 blue |
| H | Body R | 1 blue |
| I | Bird R | 1 blue |

Appliqué patterns are on
pages 82 and 83 and are
actual size and do not include
seam allowances.

"Adding a crossover pillow backing allows you to remove the insert, making it easier to store your out-of-season pillow covers. It also means your pillow inserts can be reused in another like-size pillow cover! " –Edyta

# supernova

Like a flash of light in the night sky, the exploding stars that streak across the quilt have a special glow you'll always remember.

**Quilt is 64½" × 64½"**

## fabric requirements

**Blocks:**
2 yards total of assorted dark blues for C (triangles) and E (diamonds)
1¼ yards of assorted lights for D (triangles)
1½ yards total of assorted light blues for F (cones) and G (star points)
½ yard total of light dot for H (star points)
1 yard of dark blue batik for I and J (star background)
**Background and Borders:**
4 yards of light fabric
**Binding:** ⅔ yard of blue fabric
**Backing:** 4 yards of fabric for backing
**Batting:** 71" × 71"
**Optional:** 1 package 1½"-finished Half-Square Triangle Paper (LBQ-0231)

*This quilt pattern is for advanced-level quilters. It requires accuracy in cutting and precision in sewing.*

Templates for this project on are on pages 135–137. (Position templates on fabric with the arrows on the straight of grain.) WOF designates the width of fabric from selvedge to selvedge (approximately 42" wide).

**Note:** To save time you can presew 1½"-finished triangle squares from assorted dark blue (C) and assorted light (D) fabrics using LBQ triangle paper (LBQ-0231).

## fabric cutting

**From assorted dark blues, cut:**
• 192—2⅜" × 2⅜" squares, cut once diagonally to make 384 half-square C triangles (if using presewn triangle squares, you don't need to cut these)
• 64 of Template E from assorted dark blues (16 sets of four matching pieces for each block)

**From assorted lights, cut:**
• 256—2⅜" × 2⅜" squares; cut once diagonally to make 384 half-square D triangles (if using presewn triangle squares, cut only 64 squares to make 128 additional D triangles)

**From assorted light blues, cut:**
• 64 of Template F (16 sets of four matching pieces for each block)
• 64 of Template G (16 sets of four matching pieces for each block)

**From light dot, cut:**
• 64 of Template H (16 sets of four matching pieces for each block)

**From dark blue batik, cut:**
• 64 of Template I
• 64 of Template J

**From light background and border, cut:**
• **A:** 24 of Template A
• **B:** 16 of Template B
• 8—2½" × WOF strips

**From blue binding, cut:**
• 7—2½" × WOF strips

## construction

*Use a ¼" seam allowance.*
*Press in the direction of the arrows.*

**Outer Star:**

1 Join a dark blue C triangle and a light D triangle to make a half-square triangle; trim dog-ears. Press seam allowances toward blue. Repeat to make 384 total C/D half-square triangles. You will need 24 C/D triangles for each block. Using a chain-piecing technique or LBQ Triangle Paper will speed up the process. If you're using the LBQ triangle paper remove the paper from the triangle square before next step.

2 Sew three C/D triangle squares into two units as shown. (Choose fabrics randomly to achieve a scrappy look.) Add a light triangle D to each unit as shown. Press seam allowances toward dark fabrics. Repeat to make 64 each of Unit 1 and Unit 2.

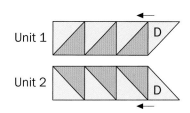

**3** (A) Sew a dark blue E piece to the end of Unit 1 as shown.

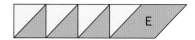

(B) Sew a light blue F piece to Unit 2 as shown.

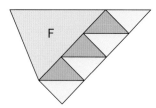

(C) Sew together the units from steps A–B following the diagram to make Unit 3; press.

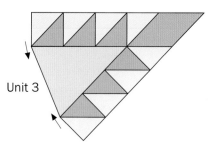

Unit 3

(D) Repeat A–C to make four total Unit 3 pieces, with matching E diamonds and matching F triangles.

**4** Repeat Step 3 to make 16 sets of four matching Unit 3 pieces total. Press and set units aside.

**5** **Eight-Point Star:** Use "Y" seams to assemble Star Centers. See "Y Seam Basics" on page 140 for detailed directions for sewing this type of seam.

(A) Sew four sets of two diamonds each using matching fabrics for each block—one light dot and one light blue. Press seam allowances in one direction.

(B) Sew those diamond pairs together to make two half stars. Trim the dog-ears. Press seams in one direction.

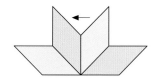 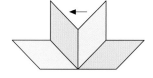

(C) Sew two half stars together to make a full star. Press seam allowances. From the wrong side, remove a couple of stitches to open the center seam allowance to allow it to lie flat (it will look like a spinning wheel).

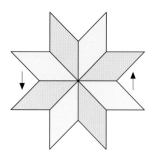

(D) Use "Y" seams to set-in the blue batik J triangles first, then set-in the blue batik I corner squares. Press seam allowances toward the star. Trim the Eight-Point Star Block to 6¾" × 6¾" if necessary.

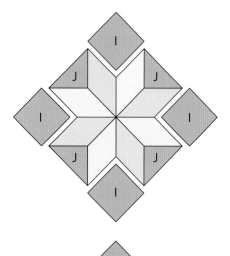

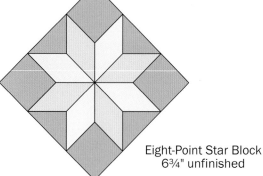

Eight-Point Star Block
6¾" unfinished

(E) Repeat steps A–D to make a total of 16 Eight-Point Star Blocks.

132 ✳

**6** **Block Assembly:**

(A) Use "Y" seams to sew one Unit 3 to an Eight-Point Star block. (You may wish to trim across the base of Unit 3 slightly from outer point to outer point to straighten the edge before joining.) Mark dots ¼" from edges to indicate beginning and stopping points for stitching. Lock the stitch as you start and stop. As you sew the pieces together, keep the Unit 3 piece on the bottom (against the machine bed) and the star on top (against the presser foot). Join pieces, sewing slowly to ease any excess fabric smoothly.

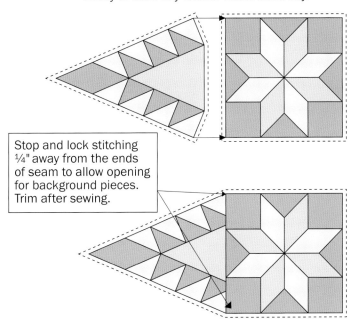

Stop and lock stitching ¼" away from the ends of seam to allow opening for background pieces. Trim after sewing.

(B) In the same manner, sew a second Unit 3 on the opposite side of the Eight-Point Star Block. Then finish the block by sewing two more Unit 3 pieces in place.

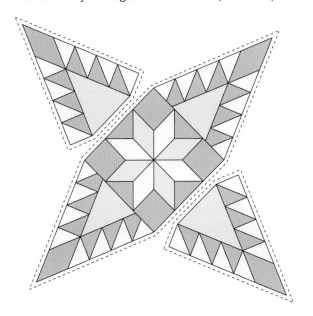

(C) Repeat steps A–B to make a total of 16 blocks.

**7** **Quilt-Center Assembly:** Lay out the pieces in four horizontal rows as shown on page 134.

(A) Using "Y" Seams, set-in the A and B background pieces to complete the blocks. Mark dots ¼" from edges to indicate beginning and stopping points for stitching. Lock the stitch as you start and stop.

(B) In the same manner, sew the blocks into rows. Then sew the rows together.

**8** **Borders:**

(A) Using the eight 2½" × 42" light border strips, piece two strips together end to end to make a long border strip. Repeat to make four long border strips.

(B) With right sides together, pin and sew a long border strip to each side edge of the quilt top. Trim excess. Press seam allowances toward the border. Repeat to add remaining long border strips to the top and bottom edges of the quilt top. Trim excess.

9 **Quilting:** Layer quilt according to the instructions on page 143. Quilt as desired.

10 **Binding:** Use the 2½"-wide blue strips to bind the quilt following the instructions on page 143.

 Take your time as you're joining blocks and rows, being careful not to stretch the bias edges. Stabilizing the fabric with a bit of spray starch as you press may make it easier to handle.

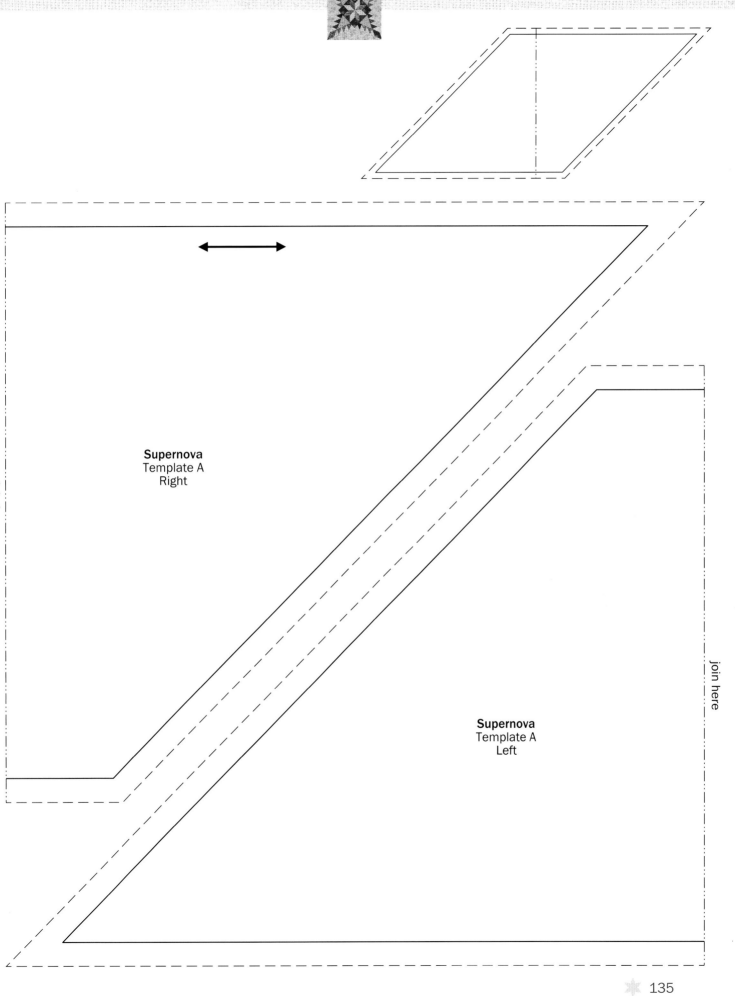

**Supernova**
Template A
Right

**Supernova**
Template A
Left

join here

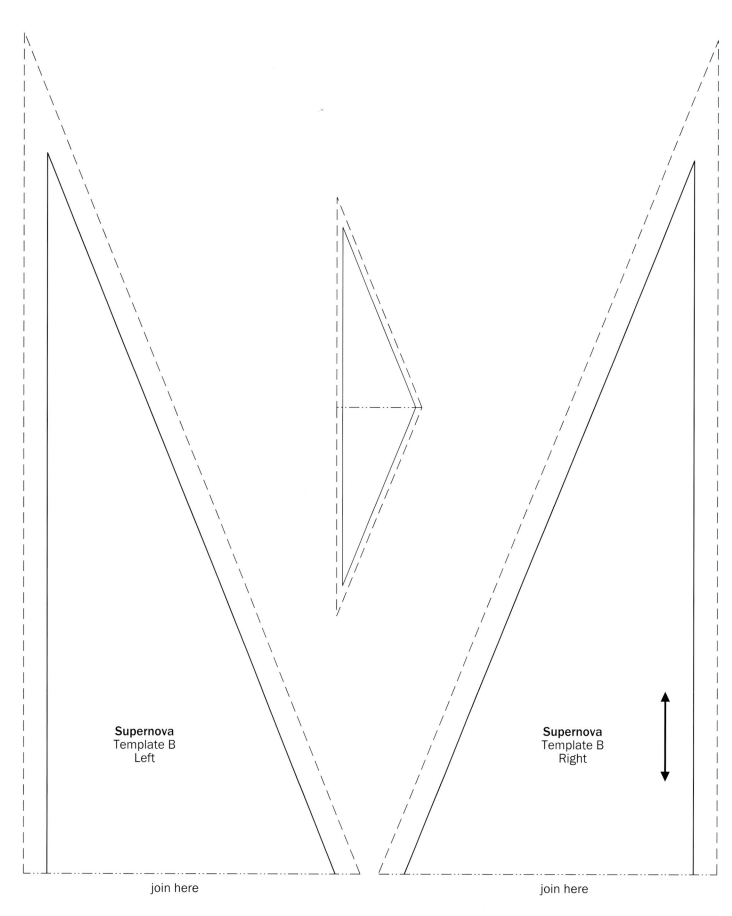

**Supernova**
Template B
Left

**Supernova**
Template B
Right

join here

join here

**Supernova**
Template E

**Supernova**
Template I

**Supernova**
Template J

**Supernova**
Template H
and G

**Supernova**
Template F

# sewing basket basics

There are many methods to assemble the patchwork and appliqué pieces in these patterns. Instructions for my preferred methods follow. Choose those that work best for you.

## appliqué options

You can use your favorite techniques to appliqué, and for your convenience, we have included three options in the instructions. But whichever method you use, please read through all instructions before starting to cut or sew. Choose your preferred assembly technique from the three listed here.

### FINISHED-EDGE FUSIBLE APPLIQUÉ

*For quick assembly, I use this appliqué technique. All shapes need to be reversed when using this method.*

- Trace your pieces onto the paper side of lightweight fusible webbing.

- Cut out shapes, leaving at least ⅛" fusible webbing around the outside of the shapes.

- Press each appliqué shape to the wrong side of desired fabric color, following webbing manufacturer's directions. DO NOT OVERHEAT FUSIBLE WEBBING!

- Cut out each fabric appliqué shape exactly on the traced lines of the fusible webbing (that is attached to the wrong side of the fabric).

- Peel the paper from the back of the fabric shapes, revealing the fusing, and place your pieces on the background fabric using the photo and layout illustration (when available) as a guide. **Note:** Dotted lines indicate where the pieces overlap each other.

- Once pieces are in place, press them gently with your iron to secure their position. DO NOT OVERHEAT FUSIBLE WEBBING! **Note:** To make the process easier, you may wish to fuse only a portion of your appliqués at one time, stopping to stitch them in place before fusing the next section.

- Prepare your sewing machine: setting should be on a small zigzag with nylon invisible thread and top tension set at 1. In the bobbin you need to use a cotton thread in the color of your background fabric.

- To secure your appliqué pieces, zigzag around all their edges, keeping the zigzag very small; most of it

should be over the appliqué piece and only one needle width onto the background right next to the edge of your appliqué.

- Make sure that your machine is not bringing up the bobbin thread to the top of your appliqué. Lower top tension if necessary; this will make your appliqué invisible. Once completed, you can gently press the block from the back, which will heal holes from your zigzag. Again be careful not to overheat. **Note:** You can use cotton thread in place of invisible thread and a blanket stitch if preferred.

**finished-edge appliqué**

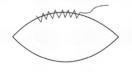

Zigzag around edge of appliqué with only 1 needle width onto block background

| | |
|---|---|
| Appliqué Edge | Raw |
| Top Tension | 1 |
| Top Thread | Nylon Invisible |
| Bobbin Thread | Cotton |
| Needle | 80 Embroidery |
| Stitch | Small Zigzag Same width and length |

## MACHINE APPLIQUÉ

*Use the full-size templates as provided to trace.*

- Carefully trace all the shapes for your appliqué onto the matte side of freezer paper. **Note:** The dotted lines indicate an overlap of shapes.

- Cut all pieces of freezer paper exactly on the traced lines. Remember to cut edges in a smooth manner; this will result in even and lovely appliqué edges. **Note:** Uneven cutting will make uneven or jagged edges on your fabric pieces.

- Choose your fabric for all pieces. Leverage the fabric color transitions in your pieces (i.e. in batiks or prints) to add additional depth to the appliqué.

- With a touch of a glue stick to the matte side of the freezer paper pattern, attach each pattern to the wrong side of your appliqué fabric.

- Next, cut the fabric carefully around the shape, leaving no more than ¼" turn-under allowance of fabric. Snip in ³⁄₁₆" on all edges, ½" apart, to allow the fabric to effortlessly fold in; be careful not to cut in too close to the freezer-paper pattern. Use the tip of your iron on a cotton dry setting to turn over the ¼" allowance of your appliqué pieces. Hold the edge over for a few seconds to allow the fabric to adhere to the shiny side of the freezer paper. Continue around until all edges are turned over. For a circle shape you will use a basting stitch around the ¼" seam allowance of the appliqué piece, and pull the stitches together, then press and hold down.

- Once all the appliqué pieces are ready, it is time to assemble the block. We will start with preparing the background space (center of your quilt top); first starch and press this area.

## HAND APPLIQUÉ

*Use the full-size pieces as provided to trace.*

- Preparation of pieces follows the same as machine appliqué.

- Once you are ready to secure the pieces to the background, use silk thread and an embroidery needle.

- Position pieces in the correct place on the background following the provided layout diagrams.

- With a small slip stitch, sew around the edges of all pieces.

### machine appliqué

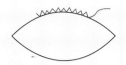

Zigzag around edge of appliqué with only 1 needle width onto appliqué.

| | |
|---|---|
| Appliqué Edge | Turned |
| Top Tension | 0 |
| Top Thread | Nylon Invisible |
| Bobbin Thread | Cotton |
| Needle | 90 Quilting |
| Stitch | Smallest Zigzag Same width and length |

- With a touch of glue, attach pieces onto the quilt top. Remember, a dotted line slips under a previous piece.

- Use your iron to press and secure all appliqué pieces in place. The shiny side of the freezer paper will allow the appliqué pieces to stick to the quilt top; use a touch of glue if necessary.

- To machine appliqué, I used Invisible Thread (100% clear nylon) with 0 tension on top, beige cotton thread on the bobbin, a quilting needle #90, and a very small zigzag stitch. As you zigzag, make sure that the needle grabs the appliqué and the background fabric alternately.

- With very sharp scissors, make a small slit in your background fabric under the appliqué pieces and remove the freezer paper.

### hand appliqué

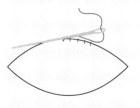

Holding needle parallel with appliqué, and using a slip stitch, grab an edge of the appliqué and a piece of background. Stitches should be no more than ⅛" apart.

| | |
|---|---|
| Appliqué Edge | Turned |
| Thread | Silk |
| Needle | Embroidery |
| Stitch | Slip stitch |

# "Y" seam basics

*Follow these steps to complete a "Y" seam. Note the dots marked on pieces. To mark dots on your fabric pieces, make a small hole in the pattern templates so you can mark directly onto the wrong sides of your fabric. Pinning at the dots to align pieces may be helpful. Starting and stopping at the dots when stitching allows for pieces to be joined at angles.*

Mark small dots on the wrong sides of your fabric where the ¼" seams meet.

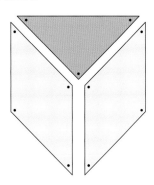

Sewing two diamonds together: Pin the seam. Start sewing at the edge. Continue stitching to the next dot, stopping your stitches at the dot. Backstitch.

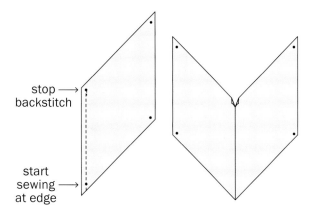

stop → backstitch

start → sewing at edge

Sewing the "Y" seam: Lock your stitch at the dot, then sew to the next dot. Stop at the dot; backstitch to lock the seam.

To join the next side, pivot the fabric, push the seam allowance between the diamonds away, and lock your stitch at the dot. Sew to the next dot, stop at dot, and backstitch.

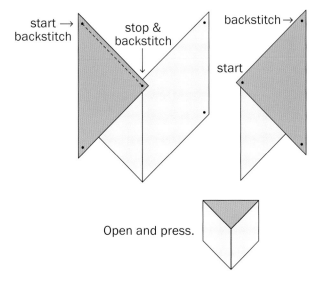

start → backstitch

stop & backstitch

backstitch →

start

Open and press.

# making templates

For several patterns, you will need to make templates of the pattern or appliqué pieces. Templates are made from durable clear plastic. Because you can see through the template material, it is easy to trace the templates accurately from the page.

Place template plastic over each pattern piece and trace with fine-line permanent marker. Note whether or not the templates have seam allowances already added.

Cut out the templates on the drawn lines. You need one template for each pattern piece or shape. Write the pattern name and letter on the template. For convenience, Laundry Basket Quilts sells several acrylic templates. If one is available for a pattern, it is noted in the project and available at www.LaundryBasketQuilts.com.

# laundry basket quilts
# half-square triangle paper

*Laundry Basket Quilts makes Half-Square Triangle Paper in a variety of finished sizes (go to www.LaundryBasketQuilts.com). Using this method, you can produce multiple half-square triangles easily—saving you time in both cutting and sewing. Depending on the package purchased, you may work with 6" × 21" fabric strips, 10" squares, or 5" charm squares. No matter which type you choose, the process is similar.*

### 1½" TRIANGLE EXCHANGE PAPER DIRECTIONS FOR 6" × 21"

**1.** Cut two fabric rectangles, 6" × 21", of light and dark fabric. Lay the light fabric rectangle on top of the dark fabric rectangle, right sides together, and then place the LBQ Triangle Exchange Paper on top of the light fabric.

**2.** Pin the paper to fabric strips, place the corner of the paper marked "Start Sewing" under your presser foot, and begin sewing on the dashed line.

**3.** Once you have completed sewing on all dashed lines, cut the triangles apart along the solid lines.

**4.** Press your triangles open, trim the dog-ears, remove the paper, and enjoy your perfect half-square triangles ready for any project.

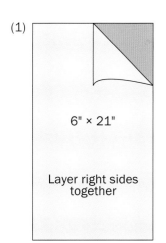

(1)

6" × 21"

Layer right sides together

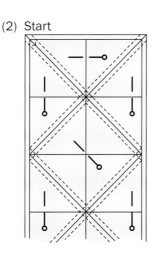

(2) Start

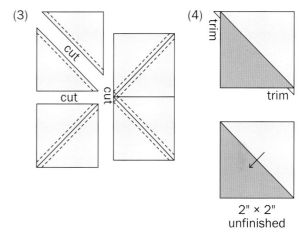

(3) cut cut cut

(4) trim trim

2" × 2" unfinished

"When sewing with Triangle Papers (available at www.LaundryBasketQuilts.com), always place the lighter fabric atop the darker one, and the paper on top of the light fabric. Doing so will make it easier to press to the dark side. After you've sewn on the dotted lines, cut them apart, and press before you remove the papers." —Edyta

## 1½" TRIANGLE EXCHANGE PAPER DIRECTIONS FOR 10" × 10"

**1.** Cut two 10" squares. Place fabrics right sides together, lighter fabric on top.

**2.** Lay paper on fabric and secure with pins.

**3.** Sew on dotted lines with a short stitch length in the direction of the arrows on the paper.

**4.** Cut on straight lines. Press block open *then tear paper away.*

**5.** Each paper makes 32—2" half-square triangles unfinished (1½" finished).

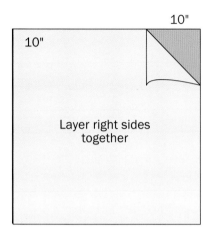

10"

10"

Layer right sides together

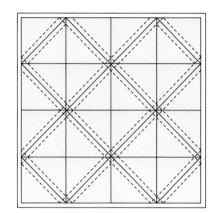

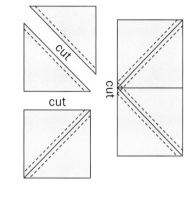

cut

cut

cut

trim

trim

2" × 2" unfinished
(1½" × 1½" finished)

# half-square triangles alternative method

*Many projects use Laundry Basket Quilts Half-Square Triangle Paper. If you prefer to make triangle-squares using the traditional piecing method, follow these instructions, noting the appropriate finished sizes at right.*

| desired finished triangle square | cut size for squares | unfinished size including seam allowances |
|---|---|---|
| 1" × 1" | 1⅞" | 1½" × 1½" |
| 1½" × 1½" | 2⅜" | 2" × 2" |
| 2" × 2" | 2⅞" | 2½" × 2½" |
| 2½" × 2½" | 3⅜" | 3" × 3" |
| 3" × 3" | 3⅞" | 3½" × 3½" |

**1.** Cut two fabric squares*, 2⅜" × 2⅜", of light and dark fabric. Cut the squares in half diagonally.

**2.** Layer one dark and one light triangle right sides together. Sew using a ¼" seam allowance.

**3.** Press your triangles open and trim the dog-ears.

*This example illustrates 1½"-finished half-square triangles. To make other sizes, refer to the chart above.*

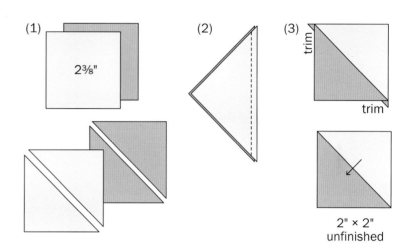

---

## quilting

*Once the quilt top is complete, follow these steps to layer your quilt and stitch the layers together. Batting and backing should be at least 6" larger than the quilt top.*

**1.** Layer your quilt in the following order:
   • Quilt backing, right side down.
   • Batting. (I prefer Hobbs for best results.)
   • Quilt top, right side up.
**2.** Baste layers together.
**3.** Quilt by hand or machine.
**4.** Trim the batting and backing even with the quilt top.

## binding

*This is the final step of finishing the edges of your quilt. Enjoy the memories you have of making your quilt and imagine how much it will be loved for years to come.*

• Sew the binding strips together end-to-end or use a 45-degree seam to create one long strip.

• Place binding strip on top of quilt front so that all raw edges align on the outside edge of the quilt. Raw edges include one binding strip edge, quilt top, batting edge, and quilt backing edge.

• Sew along the edge around the entire quilt to attach the binding to the quilt.

• When sewing, stop ¼" away from the first corner, reposition the binding to match to the next quilt side, and continue sewing.

• Fold binding strip under and then fold around the outer edge of the quilt and stitch the binding to the back of the quilt.

If the past year has taught designer Edyta Sitar anything, it's that quilting can be the respite that brings joy to the heart and mind in times of solitude. Whether at home for an extended period of time with family or tucked away at a glorious mountain cabin, she's learned to appreciate how the simplest of ingredients—fabric and threads— are at the center of her self expression.

Edyta is an accomplished author, this is her 16th book and once again she's showcasing one of her favorite hues, blue! Her newest fabric designs are available through Andover Fabrics.

The creative mind, owner, and cofounder of Laundry Basket Quilts (LaundryBasketQuilts.com) and a prolific designer of patterns and products, Edyta also teaches, travels, and speaks about quilts and quilting around the world. A native of Poland, she learned to quilt alongside her grandmother-in-law Anna. Her husband, Michael Sitar, and their three children are her dearest blessings.

*Also from Laundry Basket Quilts,*
*available at LaundryBasketQuilts.com*
*or wherever you buy books:*